Cruising
with
children

Cruising with children

GWENDA CORNELL

SHERIDAN HOUSE

This edition published 1992 by
Sheridan House Inc.
145 Palisade Street
Dobbs Ferry, NY 10522

Library of Congress Cataloging-in-Publication Data
Cornell, Gwenda.
    Cruising with children/Gwenda Cornell.
        p.   cm.
    ISBN 0–924486–27–9 : $14.95
    1. Sailboat living.   2. Family recreation.   3. Sailing—
Safety measures.   I. Title.
GV811.65.C67   1992
797.1′24—dc20
                                            92–4998
                                            CIP

Printed in Great Britain

For Muriel and Erick Bouteleux

whose company made cruising with children so enjoyable,
whether in Barbados or the Bahamas, Miami or Maine,
in Tonga, Samoa and Papua New Guinea,
Bali and Malaysia

Contents

Acknowledgements   xi
  1   The Starting Point   1

PART ONE   FAMILY LIFE AFLOAT

  2   Boats with Children in Mind   11

     Size and space   11
     Cockpit position   13
     Hull form and rig   14
     On deck   15
     Interior design   16

  3   Safe on Board   20

     At sea   21
     Harnesses   21
     In port   23
     Lifejackets and buoyancy aids   27
     Dinghy safety   30
     In the water   33
     Inside the boat   34

  4   Learning to Swim   37

     Water babies   38
     Toddlers and infants   41
     Older children   41

Drownproofing 42
Acclimatisation with lifejackets 44
Books 45

5   Child Health Afloat 46

Immediate first aid 47
    Mouth-to-mouth ventilation 47
    Burns 49
Protection from disease 50
    Malaria 50
Medical chest 51
Symptoms for which medical advice should be sought 53
Seasickness 54
Stomach upsets 55
Sunburn and heat illness 57
Skin infections 58
Nits and worms 58
Swimmer's ear and ear infections 59
Serious infections 59
Treating a child's pain 61
A healthy diet 62
Books 63

6   Babies and Infants 64

Out of the way 66
Feeding baby 67
The other end! 68
Water 69
Transporting baby 70
Amusing a small child 72

7   Making the Most of a Holiday Cruise 75

Jobs for children 76
Diaries and logbooks 81
Hobbies and interests 82
    Shell collecting 83
    Dolphin watching 84
Fishing 86
Sports 87

Contents

8   On Passage   89

      Special projects   91
      The young ones   93
      Reading   93
      Paper and pencil   94
      Games that need no equipment   95
      Board games   97
      Devising your own games   97
      Surprises and hidden treats   99
      The only child   100
      Taking it easy   101

      The Finishing Point   102
      Index   108

Acknowledgements

I am grateful to my many cruising friends whose views and experiences I have quoted in the text and to Gill Stephenson for reading and commenting on the manuscript. Peter Evans of the Edward Grey Institute, Oxford, and Denis McBrearty of the Department of Anatomy, Cambridge, both gave me valuable information on dolphin watching. Dr Peter Noble kindly checked the chapter on health. Last, but by no means least, I wish to thank my husband Jimmy for his constant encouragement, valuable criticism and especially for providing the photographs.

1
The Starting Point

When we first started cruising with our two young children, it was a relatively rare occurrence to come across other families on sailing boats. Usually such encounters resulted in the children quickly making friends, while we parents swapped stories of how we coped with family life afloat. My initial reaction in taking children to sea had been one of trepidation and I had a lot of queries. How would I amuse them on passage? What if they fell ill at sea? Would they be seasick in heavy weather? Added to such questions was the major preoccupation of a cruise planned to last several years, the problem of their education. When we set out on our voyage, my daughter Doina was seven years old, my son Ivan five years, and we planned to cruise for three years. That we only returned to England six years later with a circumnavigation of 60,000 miles behind us and children of thirteen and eleven years old, is an indication of how much we enjoyed cruising life and how all my queries had been satisfactorily resolved.

A notable change in the sailing scene over these years has been the increase in the number of parents who now take their children to sea, not only for weekends or short cruises, but also on longer voyages and circumnavigations. In a survey carried out in the Pacific in 1984 among long distance voyagers, my husband Jimmy and I interviewed the crews of fifty boats and fourteen of these had children on board, ranging in age from six months to sixteen years. This was almost one third of all the boats, whereas in a similar survey undertaken five years previously, out of fifty cruising boats, only eight had children on board. Cruising has definitely become a family affair. This book is based not only on my own experiences, but also on those of the many friends I have made who were also cruising with children, as well as the long distance voyagers interviewed for

1

The author with her children watching dolphins as *Aventura* runs gently before the trade winds in the Pacific.

various surveys.

Undoubtedly there are problems and worries in taking children to sea, but they are not insurmountable and can be solved with some thought and careful planning. The same basic principles apply at sea as on land; it is only the watery environment that is different. Careful parents take precautions to avoid accidents in the home, whether from open fires, hot saucepans or flights of stairs, so it is only an extension of this attitude to take similar precautions on a boat. Few people would let a small child unsupervised near a busy road, without being convinced that the child knew his road safety drill and was aware of the dangers of traffic. Similarly most parents apply the same principle in not letting non-swimmers near water without some supervision or protective measure such as a lifejacket. Water safety has many parallels with road safety and, regarded as such, it becomes a matter of commonsense to teach one's child to live on or near the water safely. Far fewer children are victims of boating accidents than road accidents, and if they are taught water safety and can swim well the dangers are minimised even further.

In planning a cruise with children, the questions of safety, health, boredom, occupying children on passage and their education should be thought about with the same seriousness with which one tackles the questions of route planning or provisioning. Good or bad planning in this matter can have a major effect on the success or failure of a cruise. In this book I have tried to deal with most of the facets involved in cruising with children, and although the emphasis is on long-term cruising it applies equally well to those undertaking a short cruise or only day sailing. In short, it is for any parents who consider taking their children to sea.

Before looking at these aspects, possible problems and how to deal with them, I would like to consider the benefits in taking children to sea. For most children, life at sea has a positive effect on the development of their character and independence. Sailing is beneficial to children in many ways and parents who want the best for their children should be reassured by this. In our society today we are in great danger of making life too easy for our children. The kind of upbringing, in which no expense or effort has been spared, can sometimes result in a self-centred spoilt child with little concern for others.

There is a dilemma between not spoiling a child, yet at the same time not depriving him either of what is regarded as normal by the society in which we live. A certain amount of stress is necessary for every child's development, for being short of money or denied some desired item can help a child look outwards from his self instead of inward. Overprotection of a child can lead to a smothering of a child's personality, keeping him immature and preventing the development of his independence. Sailing is one way of providing some stress and limited hardship, although within a protective setting, which will help to build the child's character and teach him to depend on himself. A similar resilience has long been acknowledged to be induced by such activities as scouting, camping, mountaineering and canoeing, while the sail training ships and tall ships that take young people on extended cruises are also regarded as character building enterprises. There is a similar effect in family cruising.

It was thoughts such as these which contributed to our decision to take our children on a voyage around the world. I did not want my children to grow up taking too much for granted, to regard as necessities what were in fact the luxuries of life. I also hoped that by sailing they would come to appreciate the basic necessities, to learn that water does not always gush out of a tap at the flick of a wrist but might have to be transported in jerrycans from the shore in a dinghy.

The limited stress or deprivation that is involved in the sailing life does not in any way imply any cruelty or lack of love. Children are very resilient beings, even the tiniest, as was demonstrated during the 1985 Mexican earthquake, when small babies survived several days trapped under the rubble. Children are much tougher than we sometimes give them credit for and will adapt to new situations and environments often more easily than adults. This is especially so if they are surrounded and supported by a caring loving family.

The importance of the family and the influence of the parents are crucial to

3

A large boat like the Norwegian *Svanhild* is an ideal playground for the younger members of its crew.

the development of any child's personality. There has been a running debate over the years about how much heredity or environment contribute to a person's development. Yet even those who place all the major emphasis on what we inherit through our genes still acknowledge that the environment a child is brought up in has a considerable effect on that child's personality. The vital role played by the family is seen in many ways, as for example in the different ways many parents behave towards their sons and daughters, which affect their development as males and females. The continuous thread of events and experiences that take place throughout each person's life from earliest childhood onward, establishes the pattern with which the individual deals with later events and experiences. Human growth is cumulative and those children who interact early with a stimulating environment have the most substance to build on as they grow up. Most educationalists are now agreed that to produce the maximum rate and extent of intellectual development, it is necessary to provide the widest range of stimulating experiences.

It is fairly obvious that being on a boat at sea is a vastly different environment to living ashore. One of the most striking differences about living on a boat is that fathers are usually much more involved with their children and their upbringing than they are ashore. This stronger role played by the father invariably has a positive effect on his relationship with the children. Living in the confines of a small boat, family life is of necessity a closer affair than on shore, maybe more in parallel with life on a farm where the whole family have to cooperate with each other to keep the farm running smoothly.

As Liz Macdonald, mother of Jeff, who circumnavigated on 31 foot *Horizon*, explained to me, 'At sea, my son saw his father Bruce actually working, coping with problems under stress, such as when gear broke in heavy weather. Before we went sailing he only saw his father for a short time at the end of each day when Bruce was tired after a day's work. Now Jeff has more respect for his father and a much stronger relationship.'

This closeness of family life and the relationship many sailing children have with their parents arises out of the fact that the child often witnesses a parent dealing with a difficult problem or even an emergency. In a squall or bad weather, a child will have to learn that the safety of the boat, and thus ultimately the safety of the family, has to take precedence over other more minor demands or fears of the child. Learning to show patience, that getting the sail down quickly is more important than whatever the child's needs are, can lead to the child considering the needs of others as well as himself.

Fear in a child is often instilled by an adult: it does not always occur naturally. Small babies have little fear of water, for example, and can be taught to swim at a young age if that fear is never promoted. Adults do not always realise that they are conveying their fears through their behaviour, for the sensitive antennae of children can pick up more than mere words. The power that can be unleashed by Nature, such as during a storm, can be frightening for anyone, let alone a child; yet if adults do not panic but act calmly in such a situation, this has an enormous influence on a child, helping him to learn to face fear and danger calmly. This is a very important aspect to help develop in a child, for panic is the cause of many accidents.

On a boat, one of the biggest environmental influences is undoubtedly Nature herself. It is almost impossible to live on the sea without coming to respect the tremendous power and force of wind and wave. Living so close to the sea, however, a child can equally wonder at the beauty of Nature in its many changing faces. By being aware of the weather, how quickly it can change, how small one is compared to the vastness of the ocean, the marine environment can stimulate a child considerably and affect his thoughts and behaviour.

When I think about all the many children I have met on long distance cruising boats, the most striking similarity between them is their independence, confidence in themselves and self-sufficiency, as compared to many children living ashore. This independence coupled with an ability to express their own opinions is the hallmark of sailing children. Part of this comes from spending time in an adult environment, but it is also due to the special features of sailing life.

Seagoing children usually make friends very rapidly, both among other boats

Friends from other cruising boats celebrate Ivan's birthday at the Royal Suva Yacht Club in Fiji.

and on shore. It always amazes me how quickly children learn to make friends, for they seem to communicate with each other more directly and simply than adults, without the hang-ups acquired over a lifetime. The friendships they make with other seagoing children have a special quality, which cuts across nationality or culture, as the similar aspects of their life outweigh the dissimilar. Equally the cruising child will often have a chance to meet children of other races, religions and languages in those children's own home environments, which is very different from meeting visitors or immigrants back home, who are often separated from their normal way of life. My children soon came to learn that children are the same the whole world over; together they laughed at the same jokes and played the same games, whether cat's cradle, hopscotch or tipping each other out of a canoe. This whole expansion of a child's world that cruising brings, both at sea and in the places visited, can only broaden a child's outlook on life.

Being a family unit, a social entity that most societies recognise, makes a difference to travelling. Without doubt it coloured our own voyage. Sailing with children on board made our reception warmer in many places, especially in the islands of the Pacific, where children are regarded with special affection. Nearer home in the Mediterranean our cruising was often made more enjoyable by the presence of our children, as during our stay in the small port of Gela in Sicily. It was Ivan's sixth birthday, and sailing along the coast of Sicily bad weather

6

Doina in a dugout canoe with newly made friends on Rendova Island in the Solomons.

hampered our plans to reach our destination. As a birthday cake had been promised, we changed our plans and put into the small shallow port of Gela. There were no other yachts in the basin, only a medium sized motor boat, and while we were battling against strong winds to manoeuvre in, a man from the motor boat launched his tender, took our lines and helped us moor alongside him. We soon learnt that yachts rarely called at Gela and he soon learnt that it was Ivan's birthday.

'How far is it into town? Is there a bus?' asked Jimmy, explaining that he wanted to buy a birthday cake.

'Don't worry, I'll take you in my car,' said our helpful neighbour.

So without further ado we sped into town, stopping in the middle of the main street while the man and Jimmy went into the baker's shop. Telling the shopkeeper to refuse Jimmy's money, the man insisted on buying the biggest and most expensive cake in the shop as well as a mound of pizzas. Meanwhile a policeman was remonstrating with the children and me about the car being parked in the middle of the main road, to which we could only reply with what we hoped were explanatory gestures. As the man emerged from the shop, the policeman's face changed.

'Ah, Signor Pino – I didn't realise it was your car – no problem.' The policeman apologised to me. Pino nodded and drove off, taking us, the cake and the pizzas to his home.

'A young son must have his birthday celebrated in a proper fashion,' he told us, as he rounded up his own children and organised an impromptu party.

During our few days in Gela, we discovered Pino to have considerable influence: closed shops were opened on a Sunday for Jimmy to buy essential spares, the children were given gifts of fruit and other things. Over drinks in our cockpit, Pino discovered that Jimmy was a journalist. His face darkened and he frowned.

'I suppose you have come to Sicily to investigate the Mafia like all the other journalists?' he queried.

'Not at all,' Jimmy smiled at him brightly. 'I'm not in the least bit interested in the Mafia, only in sailing.'

Pino smiled back and winked at him. 'You are a very wise man.'

I have recounted this episode only to illustrate some of the enjoyment that cruising with children can bring. As with many aspects of life, a lot depends on one's mental attitude. If one expects to get fun out of cruising with children, one is much more likely to find that fun than if one regards children on boats as a bore. Still, there are many things to be considered before the fun starts and those I shall be examining in this book, from the safety and health of children on board to features in boat design that are relevant to cruising with children. Ideas for getting the most out of a holiday and practical suggestions for amusing children at sea have also been included. For simplicity, throughout the book the child is referred to as masculine, although there are just as many girls who enjoy cruising. What I would like to convey above all is that cruising with children can be enjoyable and is not so very difficult. As an additional bonus it can also be of great benefit to the children themselves.

So let's go cruising!

PART ONE
FAMILY LIFE AFLOAT

2
Boats with Children in Mind

Few people buy their sailing boat specifically with children in mind, yet if one has children and hopes that they will enjoy sailing for many years to come, it is worthwhile considering certain aspects of boat design before buying a boat. If one already owns a boat, the advent of children may simply necessitate a few alterations to make the boat more suitable for a juvenile crew.

A choice of boat depends on many personal factors: where, when and for how long one plans to sail, the age and number of the crew and always of course on the size of one's wallet. Yet whether planning Sunday outings to nearby bays or a circumnavigation, certain similar points should influence one's choice. The presence of children on board has to be taken into account whatever kind of sailing is done.

Size and space

One guiding factor is the age of the children, which governs not only the amount of space they take up, but safety and protective measures as well. Although babies themselves occupy little space, they can necessitate a lot of space-consuming items, such as carrycots or pushchairs – not to speak of piles of disposable nappies, very bulky items to store. For the Canadian couple Frances and Bill Stocks, their 30 foot cutter *Kleena Kleene II* was perfectly adequate for their cruising needs until the birth of their daughter Brandi in Papua New Guinea, an event not foreseen when they left British Columbia two years previously. As we cruised in company to Indonesia, Sri Lanka and up the Red Sea, I watched their boat appear to shrink in size as the pile of baby paraphernalia grew.

We ourselves had left England with seven and five year old children happily established in the small forecabin of 36 foot *Aventura*, but by the time we were sailing in the Red Sea, Doina was a pubescent thirteen, not at all happy about sharing this small space with a teasing younger brother. A similar problem had befallen the Australian boat, *Warna Carina*, who had left home with three small children on board. By the time we met them in the Pacific several years later, on the last leg of their circumnavigation, they were accommodating three large teenagers and the family of five found their 36 foot boat rather overcrowded.

Growing children *do* take up space, often more than adults themselves, if one counts their toys, games and books. Therefore size and space are an important consideration in the choice of a family boat. Having sufficient space is also of prime importance in preventing the children getting on top of one, especially noticeable when one comes off watch tired or during bad weather. The question of size is so important that it may be worth considering buying a larger secondhand boat rather than a smaller new one if the money available is limited. I have never heard any parents cruising with children complain that their boat was too big.

When looking over a boat, it pays to envisage where the child or children are

Plenty of space is needed when friends come to play.

12

going to sleep and keep their playthings. If at all possible, the children should have a cabin of their own, preferably one you are able to shut the door on. It is very important for children to have enough space, where they can feel at home and have room to play. If it is completely separate then it does not matter too much if it gets in a mess during a passage, as this will not interfere with the running of the boat. Anyone who has come off watch at night and stumbled on a toy car or piece of building brick on the main cabin floor will know exactly what I mean. Even if a separate cabin is not available, a child should have some space for playing where a half-finished model construction or unfinished jigsaw puzzle could be left out. Even if one mainly daysails, a child is reassured by having his own bunk and territory, to which he always returns on each sail and where maybe he can leave toys from sail to sail. A contented child brings peace of mind for the parent too, so it is worth making some effort to achieve this.

On most boats, the forepeak is usually the children's province as this is conveniently out of the way and easily separated from the main accommodation. A few parents choose to designate another area for their children. When building his 40 foot *Iron Butterfly*, New Zealander Ian Hancock had cruising with his two sons in mind and allotted them the spacious aft cabin which had a large playing area, while the parents' own double berth was located amidships near to the saloon.

Cockpit position

Sailing with children may well influence the decision as to whether to have a boat with an aft cabin and central cockpit or not. An aft cabin gives some privacy to both adults and children alike, an important factor to be borne in mind. We certainly found our aft cabin a boon, as a place to retire to in order to read or sleep undisturbed when the children were playing noisily in the main cabin. Also, when the children were doing their schoolwork, Jimmy could work at his typewriter in the after cabin without either of them disturbing the other. If the cruise is going to be prolonged enough for schoolwork to have to be done, a quiet corner conducive to study should be considered. After eight years of cruising, which included a circumnavigation, the van Zelderens of *White Pointer* found it necessary to separate their two teenage children when they were studying in order to prevent them distracting each other.

If there is an after cabin, an interior throughway is much safer when small children are on board, as this means they can get into the rear cabin without having to go through the cockpit. This was a safety aspect which we did not have on our boat and the danger of a small child coming out into the cockpit was brought home to us after one sleepwalking episode at sea, fortunately when an adult was on watch. After that, in port we rigged up a bucket that clattered down noisily when the companionway doors to the cockpit were opened. This signalled to us sleeping in the after cabin that a child had come out into the cockpit.

Many parents choose a central cockpit as they feel this has more protection for small children. Our central cockpit on *Aventura* was not only deep, but was further protected by a wheelhouse, which meant that when sitting in the front corner of the cockpit the children could see out, but at the same time were sheltered from wind or rain. Whether the cockpit is in a central position or aft, the most important factor is that it is spacious, deep and well protected, especially when smaller children are on board. A raised coaming around an aft cockpit might be a design point to favour. Ideally the cockpit should be difficult for a child to fall out of. The Hantels of *Pytheas*, cruising with two young boys, had built up the sides of their cockpit so that it was very difficult for the boys to get out on deck while at sea. Another method of increasing protection is to fix canvas spray dodgers either side of the cockpit and across the stern if the design of boat features a more exposed aft cockpit. This will also help to protect a child against cold winds and exposure to the weather. Other protective measures will be discussed in the chapter on safety, which follows.

Hull form and rig

There are various points to bear in mind when considering hull form and rig. The fact that multihulls heel over less while sailing influences some parents, who feel that their children might come to enjoy sailing more quickly if they are upright. Multihulls have the further advantage of spaciousness for family cruising, although they are limited in not being able to carry so much weight. The weight capacity may be a problem for those planning to cruise further afield when the amount of water, fuel and stores to be carried is greater.

The factor of heel could also influence those who prefer to sail in a monohull to choose a stiffer boat which does not heel too much or too easily. This may mean sacrificing some speed in exchange for greater comfort. The amount of heel can make a large difference, not only to feelings of seasickness, but to games and toys staying put, not continually sliding up and down a surface when a child is playing.

The choice of the rig should be considered if children are older and keen to be involved in the sailing of the boat. Even if they are not yet old enough, a parent planning to keep a boat for some time should take into account that children might well wish to sail the boat when they do become older, and indeed should be encouraged to do so. Any of the rigs that feature a divided sail plan or smaller sails will be more easily handled by a child than a tall masted boat with large sails. This could indicate the choice of a ketch or yawl where the mizzen sail is small enough to be raised by a fairly young child. Alternatively if a single masted boat is prefered, a cutter with a staysail might be more manageable by a younger crew than a sloop.

Children enjoy being occupied around the boat, whether taking a turn at the helm, sail handling or tailing jib sheets. If they are not able to do these things because the boat is more of a racing machine, they can quickly become bored and frustrated with sailing. Whether the boat has a wheel or a tiller, it is worth considering if the boat can be steered by a child, particularly as regards visibility from the steering position. I have stood at the wheel of quite a few boats where, as an average height female, I was not able to see forward over the cabin roof easily, while a child would have seen nothing at all. A family boat should be able to be sailed by most members of the family, especially older children, and not only by the tall males on board. Similarly one can look at the winches to see if they can be operated by someone with less muscle power. In this respect self-tailing winches that can be operated with two hands might be an advantage for a young crew.

On deck

With small children on board the whole aspect of deck safety has to be considered carefully and is a function of the design. Wide side decks with high toe rails are obviously ideal where these small fry are concerned, the higher toe rail stopping toys and other little items from slipping off the side deck, as well as being safer for the children themselves. Tracks and other deck fittings should be in a position where they are not easily tripped over. Grabrails in convenient places on the coachroof are another point to look for. Many small alterations can easily be made by parents to their existing boats to improve safety for young children, such as easily reached grabrails. Canvas dodgers around the cockpit area and strong netting strung along sturdy lifelines are common measures taken by parents anxious to keep their young ones inboard. On some production boats parents have replaced the standard stanchions with higher than average ones. Laced with netting these are then taller than most toddlers, too high to be easily climbed over, and provide an effective safety barrier.

The sturdiness of pulpits, pushpits, stanchions and lifelines are other points to look for, all features which should provide something solid to hold on to when moving around the deck. If there is a gate in the lifelines, this should be checked to see if it has some form of safety clip and cannot be opened accidentally by small prying fingers.

If one is going to be getting on or off a boat with a child in one's arms or with a baby in a carrycot, it is worthwhile giving some thought to how this manoeuvre will be done. A gate in the lifelines may be one way of easing the

The sugar scoop stern on *El Djezair* was added later to the original design in order to make boarding safer and easier.

transfer of child or baby. A high freeboard on a boat can make the operation quite perilous and such boats are often difficult to climb on board from a dinghy. One solution is to have a ladder built on the stern. An increasing number of boats now have platforms or skirts at the stern and two families with children that I met in the Pacific had both recently added a sugar scoop skirt onto their existing boats. Not only does a sugar scoop transom make an excellent platform for swimming from and getting aboard from the dinghy, but one of these fathers specifically mentioned to me that he had added the skirt as a safety factor in case anyone fell overboard, making it easier to climb back on board.

Climbing in and out of hatches instead of using the companionway seems to be a universal childhood preference, so it is worth checking on how hatches open and if they can be secured properly when in the open position. It is all too easy to break the hinges of a hatch if this is not so. Many small modifications can be done on a boat to accommodate children; for example, we built a small wooden ladder onto the bulkhead next to the forward hatch in the children's cabin, with treads just wide enough to help little feet going up and down.

Interior Design

Companionway steps that are steep and narrow can be very hazardous to small children and in some boats it is a long fall from the cockpit into the boat. Ideally steps should be wide and broad with handholds at the sides easily accessible to children going up or down. Similarly inside the boat it is easy to cast a glance around and see if the handholds and grabrails function at child level or not. If not, it is a comparatively simple matter to add some suitable grabrails at a lower level or to install handholds along the side of a navigation table or in a lower position in the galley.

Even with handholds available, small children are much more likely than adults to fall over, especially in a moving boat, in the same way that they fall and trip on land, moving too fast and not anticipating changes in movement. Imagine a child tumbling down the companionway steps and take a careful look at where the child could fall. In many boats there is a sharp corner of a navigating table or galley right in the way. The simplest solution is to take a plane and sandpaper and round off all sharp corners, especially any which may be at child height.

Similarly the position of the light switches should be looked at, especially in the children's cabin and the head compartment. Often these are too high for children to reach, being on the lights themselves – a point to bear in mind if one is building or fitting out a boat oneself. Any item that children ought to be able to reach on their own without adult help should be looked at from their point of view.

When I wander around boat shows and look at boats, the lack of good storage facilities has often struck me as one of the weaker points in boat design. The forecabin, which is often the children's domain on a boat, is usually poorly provided for in this respect. With children on board the need for sufficient storage space becomes even more crucial. Having a special place for everything goes a long way towards maintaining a boat tidy and ready for sea, so that nothing can fly about if it becomes a bit rough. If one is building or fitting out a boat oneself, it is fairly straightforward to plan enough lockers, shelves and cubby holes for a family's personal requirements, but even on standard production boats extra shelving or other storage provisions can easily be added.

Children do have a knack of acquiring lots of clutter, from toys and games to pebbles, shells or interesting pieces of driftwood found on a beach. One can be strict and limit their possessions, but the more things they are allowed to take with them, the better the chance that they will keep themselves occupied and happy. One solution is to limit the children's storage to their own area or cabin, which goes a long way towards preventing an overflow into the rest of the boat, even if it does sometimes result in a child sleeping on a bunk piled high with treasures.

Fitting out *Aventura* ourselves, we built a large number of lockers and cubby holes into the children's cabin in the fo'c'sle – not that that meant it was always tidy! Small fiddled shelves above their bunks held books, while a large triangular shelf was bolted into the forepeak, over the foot end of their bunks. This large

A removable triangular shelf in the forecabin of *Aventura* provides space for additional crew.

shelf was useful for holding larger items such as board games and soft toys and could be easily removed by undoing the bolts to get at the lockers beneath the bunks.

With proper storage, it is quite amazing how much can be carried on the average boat, and many cruising boats find room for such things as folding bicycles or a second dinghy, even if only a very small inflatable. Once the children have learnt to row, it is almost essential to have a second dinghy or one can easily find oneself marooned on a boat at anchor while the children have disappeared with the dinghy, always out of calling distance. A small sailing dinghy or sailboard will also provide much fun for youngsters, sailboards being usually stored along the side deck stanchions.

Deciding what to take and what to leave behind always poses problems and the only answer is to take as much as possible. Favourite soft toys are at the top of the list, providing comfort to children away from home. Books were another item that always loaded us down, although swapping books with children on other boats kept new reading material flowing for the same amount of storage space. Flippers, masks and snorkels are items that can be stored in a wet locker or a cockpit locker along with adult diving gear. Many children enjoy fishing, so fishing tackle is another item that might have to be stored; rods are not easy to find space for, although some people fix them along a cabin ceiling.

Babies and infants also increase considerably the demand for fresh water, for

Some parents even manage to find space for bicycles.

washing saltwater out of clothes or off tender skins is more important than with adults. The water storage capacity of a boat is another item to be checked when cruising with children. The amount of water carried can be increased if required by building in additional tanks or fitting flexible tanks into other storage areas. Alternatively extra jerrycans of water can be lashed on deck, some people choosing to do this anyway on a passage as a precaution for abandoning ship.

In conclusion, the design of a family cruising boat does not have to differ greatly from other cruising boats. Ideally a seakindly boat with features of adaptable space and plenty of storage capacity might suit most family requirements. Safety features should be well to the forefront of parents' minds as well as the protection offered in the cockpit. Size, rig, and cabin arrangement are all design features that might influence the choice of a boat, as does the age and number of one's children and for how long one envisages keeping the boat. From birth to adulthood spans a fair number of years and many people may well change their boat during this time to suit the changing needs of their growing family, the ideal boat for cruising with toddlers being very different to that which might be demanded by keen teenager sailors anxious for a boat with a faster performance.

3
Safe on Board

Many of the hazards for children on a sailing boat and the ways of preventing accidents are similar to those ashore, except that the presence of water adds a potentially dangerous element. In much the same way as one educates children how to cross the road safely, so afloat one has to teach them a safety code for behaviour on the water. Instead of road sense, one instils water sense.

The responsibility for the safety of infants lies solely with the adults on a boat, but this emphasis slowly changes as children grow up, until hopefully they become responsible teenagers able to be trusted to behave safely and sensibly on the water. Concern for a child's safety however, should not lead to overprotection, as this also has its dangers. In fact, the overprotected child is more likely to have an accident, because the child has not been taught how to protect and fend for himself. The aim should be to educate the child so that he is aware of potential dangers and knows the best way to avoid them. How one approaches teaching water sense will depend on the age of the child, but even the smallest child can quickly come to understand that there are certain rules that must be obeyed. Rules can help to turn certain ways of behaviour into habits, so that the child naturally and unconsciously avoids certain hazards. The reasons for a particular rule should be carefully explained to children old enough to understand, as they invariably act in a responsible fashion once they know the reason.

At sea

On almost every sailing boat I have come across, children were never allowed on deck at sea alone or unsupervised. This applied even to strong swimming teenagers, who took watches and handled sails. It is a simple rule to make, that an adult must give the go ahead before a young person leaves the cockpit. Confining children to the cockpit at sea is a sensible principle to follow, and asking an adult for permission to go forward can quickly become a habit. If the weather is at all unpleasant or the sea rough, it is most likely that children will prefer to stay below anyway and not even venture into the cockpit, let alone on deck. Rules and conditions about when and how children can go on deck are mainly a matter of commonsense.

As children are likely to spend time in the cockpit at sea, it is essential that the cockpit is well protected, an aspect which has already been considered in the previous chapter. Some form of cockpit protection is desirable, such as a spray dodger or spray hood. A permanent wheelhouse is ideal in that it enables the child to see what is happening all around without venturing into a more exposed position. In colder climates it is important to protect children from too much exposure to wind and spray, as they get cold very easily, especially when they are not moving about. In hotter climates a wheelhouse can also protect a child from the sun, which burns a sensitive skin so much more easily on water than on land. If there is no permanent protection, a piece of canvas can easily be stretched across the cockpit and tied to the rigging to give shade from the sun.

Harnesses

Although lifejackets may be kept on board for an emergency situation such as abandoning the boat, a harness is more convenient and less bulky for a child to wear at sea. Younger children and especially non-swimmers should wear a harness and be clipped on when they want to go forward. For older children a lot will depend on the sea and weather conditions, and in poor conditions they also should wear a harness.

Under our supervision our children have often been on the foredeck without a harness, especially once they could swim and in calm conditions, either to watch dolphins riding our bow wave, help change sails or have a refreshing cold shower from a bucket. In the latter case it is wise not to let a child lean over lifelines to fill the bucket, even if it is well tied with a length of rope. As the bucket fills with water it exerts quite a forceful drag, which can easily cause the child to let go of the bucket or even lose his balance.

While older children may wear a harness only when going on deck, for active toddlers, who are much more vulnerable because of their talent for darting about quickly and unpredictably as soon as one's back is turned, the only solution is to make sure that they wear a harness and are attached even when in the cockpit. If the harness is attached to a central point, the child can move about freely to all corners of the cockpit. Preferably the line on the harness should be long enough to allow this freedom of movement, but not long enough for the child to be able to climb out of the cockpit.

For a harnessed child going on deck – and for adults, too, for that matter – a separate wire or line along the deck or on the cabin roof to attach the harness to is a good alternative to using the lifelines, where the harness has to be unclipped and clipped on again at each stanchion. One simple solution is to use a length of rigging wire, firmly attached at each end so that it lies along the deck. Another system which allows free movement right around the deck without unclipping the harness is the Latchway safety system. In this system, one of the standard lifelines is replaced with a stainless steel cable fixed by special fittings. The harness is attached by a line to a transfastener, which can then move along this cable and cross these special fittings at stanchions or rigging without coming undone.

Often a child will learn to unclip the harness and move to the next section himself. We had no special provision for harness attachment on our boat and I became concerned at the agility which my young son soon showed in unclipping himself. While this may be acceptable for an older child, I think it is preferable that a harness cannot be too easily undone by a small child. The main reason for this is that if parents are under the impression that their child is safely harnessed, they may not watch quite so closely what the child is doing and so could be unaware that he has unhooked himself from the point of attachment. One way to circumvent this is by attaching the harness with a small shackle, which can be quickly undone by an adult but not by a small child.

The manner in which the harness is fastened is one point to look for when buying a harness for a child. Another aspect is the adjustability of the harness for size as the child grows. A harness should always fit a child snugly and not be too loose. On small toddlers the harness straps can easily fall off their shoulders and it may be necessary to sew the straps together at the back to prevent this. If extra security is desired for a smaller child, a strap of webbing can be sewn on to come between the legs to secure the harness in position. As the straps of most children's harnesses adjust to fit quite large children, the manufacturers should state a weight limit for the harness, ideally printed on it as instruction leaflets are easily mislaid. It is essential that parents ensure that harnesses conform to recognised safety standards and fit correctly.

Harnesses made to standard specifications have the tether line attachment point at the back of the harness so that the child will be towed face upwards in the water. However, if a small child falls overboard when the boat is not moving but at anchor, this could result in the child being suspended with his face in the water, so in these circumstances a front attachment might be better. The wisest course is to ensure that the tethering line is not long enough to allow the child to reach the water level at all. As children's harnesses are rarely provided by charter boats, this is an important item to take along if chartering or sailing as a visitor on a friend's boat.

In port

While at sea most parents are extremely vigilant, not allowing children on deck unsupervised or making sure they wear harnesses, in port there is a great danger of relaxing one's guard as, for example, when entertaining guests in the cockpit, and not paying full attention to what a child is up to. In fact, all the cases of drowning that I have heard of have occurred while the boat was at anchor or alongside a dock. The paramount rule for safety is that non-swimmers are never let out of one's sight unless wearing a lifejacket or harness, either on or off the boat, on a dock, or wherever there is water nearby. Undoubtedly the first priority for sailing children is that they learn to swim, and this is so important that I have made it the subject of a separate chapter.

Non-swimmers may have to be harnessed as described above in port as well as at sea, although this does restrict their movement and play. Understandably many children object to being tethered like animals. When we first met Muriel

It is not only afloat but also ashore that a young non-swimmer should be supervised or wear a lifejacket. What could happen if his toy car slipped off the dock into the water?

Strong netting on *Fiu* provides extra safety for little Madeli.

and Erick Bouteleux of *Calao*, their son Fabien was an energetic two year old. Erick had fixed a length of rigging wire along *Calao*'s wide side decks and Fabien spent hours running up and down the decks working off his energy, like a dog on a lead or a zoo animal pacing up and down to the limits of its cage. The other solution for the non-swimmer is a lifejacket or buoyancy aid and that is what Fabien soon progressed to, as his parents tired of the continual pounding up and down the deck. A lifejacket can be less frustrating to a small child than being tethered.

Safety on deck can be increased by various measures, such as safety netting or higher gunwhales and toe rails, all helping to keep a child inboard. The netting should be of sufficient strength to hold a child and be laced fairly taut. Such precautions will also prevent toys from falling overboard from the deck – doubly important, as trying to recover a lost object is one of the most likely reasons a small child might fall overboard himself. Some people think that netting gives a false security, and obviously netting should not abolish the need for careful supervision of non-swimming toddlers. Yet it is one more safety precaution to back up others, and I am of the opinion that one cannot have too many alternatives to ensure that children are kept safely on board. Impressing on the child that is forbidden to climb over the netting is also very necessary.

As small children so often run when others walk, it is important to ensure that the deck surface is non-slip. Teak is best left unoiled and unvarnished to avoid becoming slippery, while patent non-skid surfaces can be stuck onto other decks. If the deck is painted, a simple method to reduce slipping is to sprinkle clean fine sand onto the wet painted surface. When dry, the excess sand can be brushed off and another layer of paint applied to fix the sand in.

Various rules can be made to lessen the chances of slipping, such as not running on deck and always keeping the feet flat. Similarly leaning over the netted lifelines for whatever reason should be banned. Children are more surefooted with their feet bare, although this has to be balanced against them stubbing their toes on any objects protruding at deck level. Checking the decks for any such hazards and keeping them clear of clutter will lessen this risk. Obviously the wearing of shoes will be governed by the climate and temperature, and any shoes worn on deck should have a suitable non-slip sole, such boating shoes now being made in quite small sizes.

Careful parents might equally well make some rules for themselves too, such as not having music or a radio on too loud when a small child is playing out of sight, so that a child's cries would not be masked by excessive noise. When boats are rafted together these smaller children must be discouraged from climbing and jumping across to another boat, sometimes difficult to enforce when they see adults and older children doing this.

Madeli Curt, eighteen months old, shows off her lifejacket, essential protection for the young non-swimmer when not being supervised.

Lifejackets and buoyancy aids

There can be no hard and fast rules for when a child should wear a lifejacket or buoyancy aid, but parents should use their commonsense, mainly considering how unsupervised or far from help the child might be and his swimming ability. For the non-swimmer, wearing a lifejacket on deck or on the dockside should be as automatic as putting on a seatbelt in a car. Under certain conditions children who can already swim might also be advised to wear some form of buoyancy aid.

Anything that is designated as a lifejacket should be able to support the child on his back with his face well clear of the water. A lifejacket should also turn a child over onto his back if he falls into the water face down or is unconscious. Any jacket that does not meet these basic requirements should not be called a lifejacket but a buoyancy aid. Because of these requirements a lifejacket has all its buoyancy on the chest and can be bulky and uncomfortable to wear for a long period, restricting play and, in hot humid climates, irritating tender skins. For children who can swim or are beginning and can at least keep themselves afloat, buoyancy aids might be considered instead. As the name implies, these are only an aid to keep a child afloat, not a lifejacket, but some of the better ones come very close to fulfilling lifejacket requirements.

There are various points to bear in mind when selecting a lifejacket for an infant or a child. For the very young it is essential that the jacket has some permanent buoyancy and does not rely on inflation by mouth or by a bottle of CO_2 gas. Some jackets have part permanent buoyancy and rely partly on mouth inflation, so if this is the case the jacket should be fully inflated when it is put on, for a child cannot be expected to blow up a jacket in the water even partially.

The permanent buoyancy of a jacket is provided either by small air-filled pockets or by foam, of either the open or closed cell type. The air-filled pockets run the risk of being punctured or chewed into, but if these are sufficiently small and numerous the loss of one or two pockets may not make a large difference to overall buoyancy. Lifejackets with large air pockets or those that depend on mouth inflation can both be rendered useless if punctured and are very vulnerable to damage, for example by chewing. The non-return valve on inflatable jackets has also been known to have been chewed off and the inflation tube similarly damaged. This possibility of damage by chewing cannot be ignored when selecting a lifejacket for the young, as it is a natural reaction for many young children especially when in distress. Some jackets contain kapok or an open cell foam in sealed compartments and both of these forms of buoyancy can absorb water if their covering is punctured. The most suitable form of buoyancy in lifejackets designed for children is that of closed cell foam, which is virtually indestructable and does not absorb water if the outer covering is damaged. The type of buoyancy of a lifejacket should therefore be ascertained before purchase. These particulars and also the buoyancy weight for which the jacket is designed

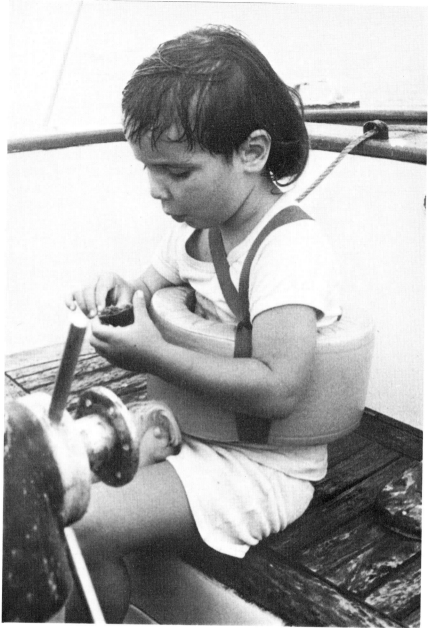

Three year old Luisa always wears her buoyancy aid when she is out on deck on *Abuelo III*.

should be available from the manufacturer and ideally should be printed on the jacket itself.

Buoyancy aids vary enormously in type and standard, some being jackets with permanent buoyancy of closed cell foam built in, while others consist of floats which tie around the body. The inflatable arm floats used in the teaching of swimming can also be considered as buoyancy aids. Again the most important points to consider are how much buoyancy there is, where it is, what it consists of and how it affects the performance of the aid. If there is not enough buoyancy on the chest, this will not turn the child over to lie safely with his face above the water. If the risk of the child falling in the water is slim, and the parent knows that the particular child is not likely to panic if he does – as in the case of a child who can swim a little and enjoys being in the water – a buoyancy aid may be a preferable alternative to a full lifejacket.

A garment for a baby must be of a type that fits the baby securely, so that he cannot wriggle out or turn around in it. One that fits like a jacket and fastens by zipping up the front with a strap between the legs to keep it in place is probably the best type. The major part of the buoyancy should be on the chest, so that the child floats face up. Some infant lifejackets have a hood or pillow padded with foam, which supports the baby's head. Similar jackets for toddlers have special flotation collars instead of hoods, which support the neck and head out of the water.

Most lifejackets for children are fixed by waist straps and webbing down the back with back buckles, designed to prevent the jacket riding up. However, many children find this type uncomfortable to wear. For this reason the waistcoat type of garment with a fabric back as used in some buoyancy aids might be preferable. Many of the jackets and buoyancy aids have crotch straps, although a few have garters or individual leg straps which children find more comfortable. Zips, simple buckles and clips are much easier to manage than ties or laces, especially for an older child who will be putting on the garment himself. Bright colours such as orange or red, which are easily seen in the water, are the first choice and some jackets have stripes of reflective tape to aid visibility. Another point to look for is that tightening of the waist straps can cause the garment to ruck into uncomfortable ridges. This will apply particularly to a slimmer child. Also the large collars of some jackets can flap about unpleasantly if it is windy. Jackets that are too long in the body can be uncomfortable when sitting in a dinghy, so a higher cut might be preferred.

It might be worth considering what the child will be wearing underneath the garment, and if there is room for bulky jumpers and jackets. Armholes large enough to take warm clothing might, however, let small arms slip out when the child is only wearing a swimming costume. Some parents require a child to also wear a harness under a buoyancy aid so if this is the case the ease with which the harness tether can be led out should be looked at. There is a limit, however, to the amount one can expect a child to wear for long periods of time and still enjoy sailing. A few buoyancy aids have a safety harness built in, which is a neat way to combine all requirements. The comfort of a lifejacket or buoyancy aid is of prime importance and will make a difference to how cooperative a child is in wearing it. In most family cruising situations a buoyancy aid is usually sufficient.

One way to feel confident about this decision is to test the aid on the child in the water. A child who is happy splashing about in the water with a comfortable buoyancy aid, or even only a swimming aid such as arm floats, can probably be left to play on a dock or boat at anchor wearing only that aid as a safety precaution without hindering his play too much. It is reassuring to test all lifejackets or buoyancy aids on a child, preferably in deep water, but failing that in a swimming pool or even in the bath for a small baby. This is the simplest way to verify that the jacket or buoyancy aid holds the child in the safe and correct position. A small child can also be given confidence this way if he realises that he will not sink when wearing the jacket, and this can help reduce the child's fear of water, increasing the chance that he will not panic if he should fall into the water accidentally.

Dinghy safety

Even after a child has learnt to swim, many parents insist on a lifejacket or bouyancy aid being worn in the dinghy, particularly in sailing dinghies or when the child is without an adult. Novice swimmers and younger children can go along with other children quite safely if they are lifejacketed. Almost without exception children afloat enjoy taking off in a dinghy independently to explore the little creeks and backwaters of an anchorage. At some point in their growing up, children have to be trusted to go off on their own and behave sensibly, and obviously this point will vary from child to child. It will also depend on where they plan to go, weather and sea conditions, state of the tide and how well they can row, sail or drive the outboard on the dinghy. The strength of the wind and any tidal currents must be carefully considered, so that there is no danger of the dinghy being swept away, because the child does not have sufficient strength to row against the wind or tide.

Most children enjoy learning to row and quite rapidly become proficient, even if sometimes unorthodox, rowers. It is worth spending some time teaching them a good rowing stroke, letting them practise while you are also in the dinghy or nearby until you are satisfied with their proficiency. Some small children find it easier to learn to scull with one oar as they can use both hands for this and so get more power behind their stroke than with an oar in each hand. My son taught himself to propel our dinghy quite fast by a one oared paddle stroke from the bows, which he invented himself. Even if normally rowing with two oars,

Non-swimmer Benedict Hantel (3) wears a buoyancy aid whenever he goes off in the dinghy with his elder brother Eric (7).

it is worth practising one oared propulsion too, for those occasions when an oar might be broken or let adrift. Rigid dinghies, whether made from wood, aluminium or fibreglass, are much easier to learn to row than an inflatable, and with children on board it might be worth ensuring that the tender is lightweight and easily rowed. Similarly a sensible eight or nine year old can manage a small outboard engine, provided he has been taught properly – again parents will make sure the child knows what he is doing before letting him out of sight.

If an outboard engine is used, needless to say, oars should always be included in the dinghy in case of engine failure. Similarly a bailer of some description should be carried in any dinghy, however it is propelled. If the outboard starts with a pull cord, some children may need to use both hands to pull it in order to raise sufficent force. As a safety precaution it should be a rule that passengers always turn their faces away from the cord being pulled. If the cord does not remain attached to the engine after it has been started, it should be tied onto something in the dinghy, such as the handles or seat, to ensure that it does not get lost. If they have a choice parents might be advised not to have the open-topped type of outboard engine, for an insufficiently pulled cord can flick back with the child's hand, or a girl's long hair could be accidentally wound in. The closed-topped engines where the starting cord retracts out of sight into the casing are to be preferred when being operated by a child. When an engine is used, the

31

danger of trailing anything in the water, such as towing a toy, should be emphasised as it could become entangled in the propeller. For the same reason making sure the painter is safely inside the boat should become a habit.

General dinghy behaviour for small children should begin with the rule of sitting still and not rocking the boat unnecessarily. Keeping feet and fingers inside is important especially when coming alongside a dock or boat. Not putting the feet or hands between the boat and the quay or dock applies not only to the dinghy but for all kinds and sizes of boats, as a sudden lurch or jolt can so easily crush fingers or feet. Never jumping into the dinghy and being careful not to push a dinghy away with one's feet as one clambers aboard a boat are other principles worth insisting on. Mastering the correct knots intrigues most children and they often become quicker and more adept knot makers than adults. This will ensure that the dinghy is always tied safely alongside or behind a boat or dock and will not come undone. For smaller children, tying both the bow and stern on short painters can make getting in and out of the dinghy easier. Nearly all the points about dinghy behaviour are commonsense, but it is worth pointing out the reasons for any rules, especially where outboard engines are concerned.

Getting on and off a boat from or into a dinghy can also be hazardous when carrying a baby or small child. The first requirement is for the dinghy to be tied firmly fore and aft so that it cannot move far away from the side of the boat. A baby can be carried either in a sling close on the chest, which is best for tiny babies, or in a carrier on the back, more suitable for the older infant. These baby carriers do leave the hands free for climbing on board, and if one is alone they are probably the best solution. For a two handed operation, there is the alternative method of transferring a baby to the boat in a solid carrycot on the floor of the dinghy and handing this cot up onto the deck, usually through a gate in the lifelines. The same principle is involved as in transferring boxes of stores or any such item, and the main danger is pushing the dinghy away from the side of the boat as one lifts the baby or child up to the other person on the deck.

The positioning of cleats on deck or the choice of fastening points for the dinghy will vary from boat to boat and everyone has to work out the safest way to board their particular boat, the height of the topsides being a crucial factor. Snaphooks fitted to the optimum length of line on bow and stern painters can make this operation quicker. Boarding ladders should always be firmly fixed so they cannot slide or shift about too much (this also prevents damage to topside paint). A skirt, platform or permanently fixed ladder on the stern was mentioned in the previous chapter on boat design, and these features do make boarding safer.

In the water

Most of the children brought up on and around boats turn out to be good swimmers, and those who sail in warmer waters are usually like fish, spending as much time in the water as on the boat. When they reach this stage many of the rules regarding lifejackets or dinghies obviously go by the board, as children play at capsizing dinghies for fun or deliberately fall over the side of the boat. Pushing another person who is not expecting it into the water, however, should always be discouraged.

Dangers in the water are the same for children as for adults and it is wise to make sure that children are aware of them. Attention should be paid to any undertows or currents that may exist where the children are likely to be swimming and they can be warned to stay away from obviously dangerous areas. Care should be taken to keep out of the way of fast speed boats and water skiers as soon as these engines are heard, for sometimes the drivers of such boats are not very attentive or aware of swimmers, particularly if they are snorkelling or under the surface. In many places there are strict restrictions about where one can water ski, yet occasionally I have seen water skiers weaving in and out of boats at anchor, regardless of children playing in the water. In one case the culprits were teenagers from one of the anchored boats, clearly having not been taught water sense by their parents.

A visit to an aquarium might be an easy way to show a child animals that are to be avoided if seen in the water. The excellent Suva Aquarium in Fiji has special displays arranged to show the dangers that lurk in the sea. Tropical waters appear to contain more such perils than temperate waters but, even so, poisonous animals are not all that common – no more than snakes, scorpions or tarantulas on land. One precaution that children can be taught is to be careful where they put their hands and feet, and especially not to put them into holes where they cannot see what is inside. Some creatures such as eels love to hide in dark holes and can bite if surprised.

From the moment they start swimming children should be encouraged to keep their eyes open underwater, and wearing a mask or goggles can help them to do this. Any creature that is not known or recognised should be treated prudently and with caution. Some of the most important animals to avoid are jellyfish of all types, stone fish, which lay motionless looking like stones on the seabed, and certain cone shells, which can release a poisonous dart. Large clams with attractively coloured tentacles can quickly shut tight over exploring fingers or careless toes and so should be given a wide berth. Prickly sea urchin spines are difficult to remove from feet and easily get infected if they are left – one of the reasons for wearing plastic sandals while reef walking, beachcombing or playing in shallow water.

It is, however, sharks that spring to most people's minds when they think of dangers in the water, although barracudas and eels can also give a nasty bite. In most anchorages or harbours, the possibility of sharks will be well known by local people and their advice should be sought. Fortunately the more dangerous sharks do not usually frequent enclosed lagoons and shallow waters but tend to stay on outer reefs and in the open ocean. Although not all species are equally dangerous and small lagoon sharks rarely take much notice of a swimmer or diver, sharks must always be treated very warily and certain rules must be obeyed in unknown waters. Sharks like to cruise where their dinner is, so they are usually to be found where there is plenty of fish. Swimming near any fish factory, processing plant or close to fishing boats where fish are being gutted should be avoided. For similar reasons any fish caught while spearfishing or with a net should never be carried near to the body but put immediately in a dinghy or on shore. Sharks feed at dusk, so that is the time of day to be cautious about swimming in unknown places; early morning or midday are much safer times. Another golden rule in shark suspected areas is never to dive or swim with a cut, wound or while menstruating, for blood attracts sharks, as does splashing or flailing about.

A general principle in water safety is to teach a child to stay calm and not panic if anything unusual happens. A panicking child is much more likely to come to harm and even drown as he gasps for air than the child who remains calm. Parental example is the key, for a parent who stays calm will generate confidence in the child too. Once while our children were swimming in a lagoon in the outer Bahamas, a shark appeared on the scene. It showed no interest in the swimmers, but of course Jimmy told the children to swim calmly to the dinghy and get in, while he stayed between them and the shark, holding his diving knife which he always wore strapped to his leg while swimming. This the children did without the slightest fuss or panic, because they already knew that splashing or making a noise might attract a shark more than normal swimming. They also knew that sharks rarely attack without first inspecting their prey, because we had discussed sharks and their habits with them when we first started cruising in tropical waters.

Inside the boat

Safety inside the boat has many parallels with safety in the home – for example, making sure that medicines are locked away or out of reach and that poisonous fluids or compounds are not stored in accessible places. Anything that could be poisonous should never be put into old lemonade or soft drink bottles.

A toddler will have to be watched all the time on a boat, not only to prevent injury to the child, but also to ensure that inquisitive fingers do not wreak havoc with expensive marine equipment. It is worth spending a few minutes looking around one's boat, maybe even on one's knees at child level, in order to assess what could be a hazard for a child. Where would a child be likely to fall from, the pilot berth or the companionway steps? A sensible rule to make is that a child never climbs up or down the steps with a toy in his hand, so that both hands are kept free for holding on. Are there any projecting corners in the fall path of the child? These can easily be rounded off, so that any fall results in bruises not nasty lacerations. How do the stopcocks in the head operate? Could an unwatched child accidentally flood the boat? Are there any moving parts in an accessible place on the boat that long hair or clothing could get caught in? These are some of the questions that might arise from looking around a boat from a small child's angle.

Whether one cooks by kerosene or gas, the cooker is one item to be particularly careful about allowing children near. Playing with the taps of a stove should be strictly forbidden, even if these are of the fail-safe variety. A turned on tap can easily release kerosene over the galley floor, while the danger of an explosion from released gas is very real. Although considering general safety inside a boat mainly in relation to toddlers, the correct use of bottled gas has to be learnt by all, young and old. The safest precaution is to always turn off the gas at the bottle as well as at the stove. This was the rule on our boat and it soon became second nature. The gas was turned off at the bottle and so the pipe to the cooker emptied of gas before being turned off there as well. In this way the danger of an explosion is minimised. Gas can be quite safe if used properly.

Saucepans should always have their handles turned away from the edge, so that a child cannot grab or pull a saucepan over. Saucepans with lug handles are much safer on a boat as the handles do not project. The top of the stove should be fitted with pan holders into which the saucepans fit snugly. When cooking in a seaway, it is safer to use the oven if possible and important to keep children well away from the pouring of any hot liquids. Children should be sitting down in a secure position when they eat so as to lessen the chances of them upsetting hot food over themselves. Young children should not be given too hot food; it is better to wait for it to cool slightly before serving it out. The only accident we had during 60,000 miles of sailing was when Ivan tipped a bowl of hot custard down his bare chest in his impatience to eat it. It might be better to serve such food in a mug with handles rather than in a bowl, if it is to be held in the hands and not eaten at a table. If a small baby or infant has to be fed, it is safer to do this with the child on one's lap so that parent and child move together with the movement of the boat.

Writing about accidents and safety always seems rather horrific, whether one is considering gas explosions, sharks or falling overboard. Yet similar dangers exist on land too, in the home or on the streets, and the most important point is to teach a child to be aware of these dangers and how to act sensibly to avoid them. Overprotection bears the risk that the child does not have a chance to become independent and think for himself, yet this should never be confused with valid protective measures which need to be taken. Making sure that a toddler who is unable to swim is never near water unsupervised or without a lifejacket is not overprotection, but very necessary protection indeed. I have often been impressed by how sensible sailing children can be, their independence and maturity often marking them out from their land based counterparts. Until they reach that stage, however, the smaller ones will require the utmost vigilance and in this field parental responsibility cannot be shirked.

4
Learning to Swim

One of the first priorities for any parents considering taking their children to sea or even near the water is to ensure that they can swim. It has now been well established that it is possible for babies to stay afloat even before they can walk, so no age is too young to begin learning to feel at home in the water. The accent in this chapter is on gaining confidence in the water and keeping afloat, drownproofing as opposed to learning swimming techniques or specific strokes. The aim is to ensure the survival of a child who accidentally falls in the water, not to produce an Olympic champion.

I have twice been in the vicinity when children drowned, one a sixteen year old non-swimmer who was fooling around on a windsurfer close to a beach, and the other a two year old girl playing unsupervised on a dock and not wearing a lifejacket. I am continually surprised at the number of parents who cruise with their children and who have not made the effort to teach them to swim at an early age. Among fourteen long distance voyagers interviewed in the Pacific who had children sailing with them, eleven out of the total of twenty children could not swim properly. These were mainly the younger children, some of whom were in fact in the process of learning. Only one of these eleven non-swimmers wore a buoyancy aid or lifejacket as a matter of course; two wore harnesses at sea but not in port, their parents claiming to be always vigilant, while another young non-swimmer only wore his lifejacket when his parents were not supervising him, for example when he was rowing in the dinghy with his elder brother.

I was amazed to be told that one of the non-swimmers, a six year old, had already been fished out of the harbour twice and still his parents did not insist

Mareva (4) and Jimmy (6) feed the ducks from the deck of *Vahine Rii*. With children who cannot swim one must be more careful in harbour than at sea.

on him wearing a lifejacket; nor did they appear to be making any effort to teach him to swim. In my mind this kind of attitude amounts to criminal negligence. Effort is the key word, because that is the main requirement needed: a frequent and regular effort has to be made by the parent, devoting time to the task in hand. In contrast to the example quoted above, on *Swan II*, further along the quay in the same harbour, Nicky Samuelson, also six years old, had been swimming since she was seven months old and at the age of three had even been offered a place in a junior swimming team – demonstrating the result that a little effort can produce.

Most of the progress in teaching the very young to swim has come from the warm climes of California and Australia, where garden swimming pools are commonplace and many parents fear for their toddlers' safety. Virginia Hunt Newman in the United States and Claire Timmermans in Australia are two of the teachers who have pioneered techniques for teaching babies to swim and both of them have written useful books on the subject.

Water babies

Babies are not born being afraid of water: this fear is only developed from adult behaviour and attitudes. In fact newly emerged from the wet and watery womb, babies are quite happy lying in warm water even from a few days after birth. The first steps in helping a baby to feel at ease in water can be taken at home in the bath tub on a regular basis, in clean warm water before any soaping or shampooing begins. The baby should never play in soapy water because this can get in his eyes and so make him associate water with unpleasant symptoms. Ideally once a day, but at least three times a week, a consistent programme should be followed, because regularity and frequency are important for a small child with a short-term memory. Professional teachers consider it even more effective if the parent actually gets in the bath with the tiny baby. Even with the youngest baby it is advised to use the normal bath tub and a reasonable depth of water, so that the child gets used to a larger volume of water.

The main principle is that water play should be fun, something to be enjoyed, which is not too difficult to convey to the normal child splashing and playing with his toys in the water. The first step is to start trickling water over a baby's head and face from a sponge, gradually increasing the amount over the eyes. Supporting him under his neck and holding one leg, the baby can be floated on his back, gently moving him backwards and forwards. The support given to the child can gradually be reduced over a period of time. When the baby is used to this floating, he can be moved so as to make waves, letting them ripple over his head from the top, not from the feet, so that water does not flow into his nose.

Also as a game the baby can be playfully dunked up and down in the water, blowing onto his face all the time as he goes under. The main purpose in this type of play is to get the baby used to having water over his face and not to mind. When this is achieved the baby can be submerged for an instant; by a natural reflex he will hold his breath. This submersion time can be gradually increased over the weeks until it lasts several seconds. The reason for blowing on the face until the child goes under is that this causes the baby to shut his eyes and naturally hold his breath. It also becomes a signal that he is about to go under.

When the baby is happy about getting his face wet, one can progress to holding him front down in the water encouraging him to kick and splash. Supporting the child under the chin and tummy, he can be similarly submerged for a few moments. Always make sure that both nose and mouth are either out of the water or both totally submerged, so that the baby will not try to breathe underwater, as might happen if either nose or mouth only are submerged. Another game is to blow bubbles into the water, babies learning to copy their parents quite easily. All of these exercises should be made into fun, and if a child is upset by any of them do not insist, but return again to the beginning and just play or trickle water. Never force a child to submerge if he is obviously very unhappy about it.

The next step is to lay the baby under the water on his front, supporting him under the chin and tummy and letting him kick his legs and paddle his arms as he will probably do instinctively. By slight pressure under the chin, the baby's

39

head can be brought to the surface so that he takes a breath. This is repeated often, so that pressing on or lifting his chin becomes a signal for coming up for air. All the time the baby should be encouraged and praised and the sense of enjoyment maintained.

Once the baby has gradually become used to submersion and water play in the bath, it is time to progress to a pool. This is where more effort will be needed, for finding a learner's pool that is both warm and shallow is not easy in many areas. A temperature of 26–32°C (80–90°F) is recommended for young beginners, and for small babies it should ideally be nearer 32° (90°C). Often public swimming pools are below this temperature, and if there is no alternative pool the lesson time should be reduced and the baby got out of the water into a warm towel quickly at the end of the lesson. Learning to swim in a warm climate has obvious advantages in that a suitable pool is more easily found. If no pool is available, continuing to play and submerge in the bath will still have an advantage in making a baby happy about water and will make swimming easier later on when the time comes.

For the first experience in a pool, the baby should be taken in gently held in his parent's arms and then the same kind of games that were played in the bath, blowing bubbles, dunking and splashing, can be gradually started. If the baby is laid in the water on his front and moved along, he will automatically make movements similar to those of crawling on land. To encourage the child to open his eyes underwater, some coloured non-floating toys or objects can be placed on the bottom of the pool and the child encouraged to search for them.

The main emphasis is for the baby to feel at home in, and especially under, the water. From then on, the amount of support under the baby can be gradually reduced and the submersion time increased. The baby should always be guided up by the chin to the surface in order to breathe, but this pressure can become lighter and lighter as the reflex of coming to the surface for air is established. The aim, eventually, is to release the baby completely under the water. Similarly the baby can be dunked up and down, again blowing on his face all the time until he goes under to encourage the holding of the breath. Some time should also be devoted to floating the baby on his back with his arms outstretched. Younger babies can often learn to float more easily this way than older babies, because over nine months or so a baby will become more interested in what else is happening all around him, and may wriggle, move his arms or try to turn.

No attempt to teach swimming strokes should be made and only the natural doggy paddle encouraged. This underwater method seems strange to many adults who learnt to swim in a different fashion, but it is the more natural method for babies, perhaps more akin to the womb they came from. The purpose is to waterproof the child, so that an accidental tumble into water will not automatically result in a gasping and panic-stricken child struggling to keep his head above water, which can in turn result in much more rapid drowning

40

unless the child is speedily rescued. Proper swimming strokes and improvement in technique can be learnt in good time when the child is older.

Toddlers and infants

An infant can be taught to swim using the same techniques as described for a baby and can also begin by having fun in the bath with splashing, face-wetting and dunking under the water. Again the aim is for total submersion, the natural underwater method. In some respects it is a little easier once a child can talk and also understand verbal directions more readily, although the child might already have developed some aversion to water. In the pool, familiarisation with water can progress in the same way until a child can do a basic underwater doggy paddle and float on his back.

Before moving on to actual swimming the child must learn to breathe out underwater, because a baby or small child automatically holds his breath when submerged. This can be taught in the bath tub or in a bowl, as a game of watching the bubbles rise. In shallow water where the child can keep his hands on the bottom while his legs float on the surface, he can take a breath, submerge his face and breathe out naturally blowing bubbles. As well as in the bath, this can be practised in a shallow pool or even in the sea off a beach. If the seawater is warm enough, there is no reason why all of this learning cannot take place in the sea when a pool is not available.

Jumping up and down in the water while holding onto the parent's hands and eventually submerging, is another way of playing a game that gets a child used to submersion, encouraging the child to jump higher out of the water and sink lower underneath with each jump. Learning to jump from the side of a pool into the water towards a waiting adult also instils confidence.

Once the child has learnt to float unaided on his back, swim a rudimentary doggy paddle, and is happy about total submersion, able to keep his eyes open underwater and breathe properly, then teaching can progress to swimming on the surface and learning different strokes, using buoyancy aids such as float boards.

Older children

For children who have not learnt to swim early and may have developed some fears or apprehension about total submersion in water, the natural underwater method will probably have little success. In this case it may be better to begin teaching with the aid of inflatable arm floats or other forms of swimming aid.

Most arm floats are made of a plastic material, having two compartments which can be inflated separately. Fully inflated and pushed on the arms above the elbows, these floats will keep a child on the surface with the minimum of movement from arms and legs. They are ideal for giving the non-swimmer confidence in the water. An older frightened child can even wear two floats on each arm to give him the initial confidence that he is not going to sink under. The child should be taught to propel himself along by kicking his legs, on both his back and his front, and also be encouraged to float on his back with arms and legs outstretched. As the child learns to float and doggy paddle, the arm floats should be removed as soon as possible so that he does not become too dependent on them. This is best achieved by progressively deflating first one of the two compartments on each arm and then the second compartment. As the air is released a little more at each swimming session, the child's confidence grows as does his ability to move his arms in a better fashion without the hindrance of the floats. Once this confidence is established the arm floats can be finally discarded.

If a child learns to swim on the surface with the aid of arm floats, it is important not to neglect giving him underwater experience, so lots of face wetting, head ducking, blowing bubbles and opening the eyes underwater should also be included. This mental barrier of being unwilling to submerge completely and voluntarily is the biggest obstacle to becoming a true swimmer. If an older child has a phobia about submersion, one good way to build confidence is to practise immersion in a bowl containing only a few inches of lukewarm water. The child should get used to immersing his head, at first pinching his nostrils if he wants to and then progressing to blowing air out underwater and opening his eyes. When some confidence has been established using the bowl, he can try the same thing in the bath before progressing to trying it in a pool. The next stage is to help the child to float on his back and his front without moving his arms and legs unnecessarily. Once he can discover that he does not sink automatically, he will be at the point of overcoming his main difficulty in becoming a swimmer.

Drownproofing

The idea of drownproofing originated with Professor Fred Lanoue of the Georgia Institute of Technology. It is basically a floating technique for keeping alive in the water with the minimum of effort and can be taught to any children who are old enough to understand what is required. It is not necessary for them to be proficient swimmers to learn the technique.

The basic float position is on the front with the head submerged, the arms loosely forward and the legs hanging down. The majority of children will find that with their lungs full of air they have a natural buoyancy and can just hang in this fashion with no effort at all. In order to breathe, all that has to be done

Arm floats can be used as a buoyancy aid, as well as giving confidence in the early stages of swimming.

is to exhale into the water, still keeping the face down, then lift the head upwards out of the water by giving a little movement of the arms. A good breath is taken and then the face dropped back into the water. The cycle is repeated and, as the body is in a resting position using little energy, the person does not get so tired but can keep this up for a long time. The main reason for keeping the head down and submerged is that it is proportionately one of the heaviest parts of the body; a considerable effort is needed to keep its weight above the surface, so it is better to let the water support it.

In practice a major factor in survival, just as much as any technique mastered, is the temperature of the water. Although survival time is very short in cold water, in the tropics the sea is often at a temperature where prolonged survival is possible. A few years ago, sailing among the Gilbert Islands, the crew of a New Zealand catamaran fished out of the water a small girl who had been washed out to sea from a nearby island while fishing on the reef. She was semiconscious, but had survived two days in the water by naturally adopting a survival position curled up like an embryo. In many Pacific islands children have always been taught to swim as babies in similar ways to those outlined above. The catamaran took her back to a village already mourning her death.

In colder waters some insulation is provided by clothing trapping a layer of air, and beginners should not be encouraged to try to remove their clothes in the water. As wet clothing out of the water will weigh heavily and create a drag, they

43

should be taught to keep all parts of the body that are covered by clothing underwater to help them stay afloat. Survival techniques, such as removing clothes, knotting ends of trousers and sleeves and then blowing the clothes up into bouyancy bags, which are taught by some swimming teachers, should only be practised by children who are already proficient swimmers.

Acclimatisation with lifejackets

If a child has not learnt to swim, but wears a lifejacket or buoyancy aid on the boat or while playing on a dock, it might be worthwhile putting the child into water out of his depth with this garment on, the parent remaining close at hand. Firstly, this will give the parent the reassurance that the aid is able to do the job it was purchased for and support the child in the water. Secondly, it will give the child confidence that he is not going to go under in deep water. It is important to do this in water where the child cannot touch bottom and an ideal place is around the boat while at anchor. This will help a child not to panic if he does accidentally fall in. Even after my children and their friends could swim well, they still sometimes chose to play in the water with their buoyancy aids on, lazily basking on the surface with the minimum of effort.

In very hot climates a full lifejacket can be very irritating for a small child to wear, especially a child with sensitive skin, and some parents use the arm floats as an alternative under these conditions. Again it is important to discover how the child behaves in deep water with the arm floats on, because these are only an aid to swimming and not a lifejacket. However if the child is happy and accustomed to being in the water with the floats on, these may be sufficient to save him if he accidentally slips off a dock or a boat while playing.

The emphasis in this chapter has been on making children safe in the water, not on any swimming proficiency. If a parent feels unable to teach his child, there are many professional teachers who make a speciality out of teaching the very young to swim. Yet most of these teachers agree that the parent is the best person to undertake the task if possible, because of the natural confidence that a small child has in his parents. The guidelines in this chapter are of necessity fairly brief and greater detail can be found in specialist books on the subject of teaching swimming, which are well worth consulting. Regular and constant effort is undoubtedly needed, but it will be well rewarded, because there is a clear peace of mind that comes when one's child is equally at home in the water as he is on dry land.

Books

Lanoue, Fred. (1978) *Drownproofing: A New Technique for Water Safety*. New Jersey: Prentice-Hall, Inc.

Hawley, Anne. *Swim, Baby, Swim*. London: Pelham Books.

Meredith, Susan. *Teach Your Child to Swim*. London: Usborne Publishing.

Newman, Virginia. (1985) *Teaching an Infant to Swim*. New York: Harcourt Brace Jovanovich.

Timmermans, Claire. (1990) *How to Teach Your Baby to Swim*. Scarborough. House.

5
Child Health Afloat

Dealing with a sick child or coping with a medical emergency while away from professional help is a natural worry for parents thinking of cruising with their children. In some respect they may be encouraged, because a child is less likely to catch common infectious diseases on a boat than on shore. Nevertheless accidents can happen or a child can fall ill, and the wise parent will make some preparations for such an event. Even if one does not sail very far offshore, it may still be several hours after an accident before professional help can be reached, and some knowledge of what to do in an emergency can save a life or lessen injury. The most obvious case when immediate action is vital is when a child has stopped breathing after falling in the water. Those planning an extended cruise out of the range of normal medical assistance have to be prepared to deal with a much greater range of problems. Taking a short first aid course as part of the general preparation for cruising would never go amiss in dealing with both adult as well as children's emergencies.

The first step in allaying fears is to have a good book at hand. There are various first aid manuals available, some having been written especially for yachtsmen, such as Peter Eastman's *Advanced First Aid Afloat* or Dr Counter's *The Yachtsman's Doctor*. However, these books deal mainly with adult problems, although many of the essentials could also apply to children. St John Ambulance publish a delightfully simple and clear *The Essentials of First Aid*, which is used to train young first-aiders such as cadets, scouts and guides. I also had on my bookshelf *The Ship Captain's Medical Guide*, published by Her Majesty's Stationery Office, for merchant ships not carrying a doctor. This is a very comprehensive book packed with information, and although dealing with the problems of merchant seamen, such as drunkenness and venereal disease, it does have very clear tables for diagnosing the causes of abdominal pain, unconsciousness, or the differences between measles, German measles and scarlet fever. The signs, symptoms and treatment of all major diseases are clearly laid out so as to be understood by a layman. The book deals with many matters that particularly appertain to life at sea and in port, such as checking on the purity of water supplies. For the common illnesses and problems of childhood there are many manuals on child care written for parents.

Having bought a book, it is essential to look through it before consigning it to the bookshelf and particularly to read the sections on essential first aid. In an emergency it is usually vital to act quickly; there may not be time to wonder where one has put the first aid book or to thumb through the pages looking for the section that is relevant. Once the essentials have been dealt with, the book can be consulted at one's leisure for further treatment or procedures.

Immediate first aid

There are three major priorities in an emergency:

(1) To restore breathing.
(2) To stop major bleeding.
(3) To move the patient out of danger.

If a child has stopped breathing, it is essential that resuscitation is started immediately, even if the child is also bleeding or in an exposed position. Obviously if breathing has stopped due to immersion in water, the child has to be got out of the water first; but if, for example, the child has been knocked out by the boom and is lying unconscious and not breathing on the side deck, artificial respiration should be begun at once before moving the child into a safer place.

Stopped breathing does not necessarily mean death, but the brain can only function for a few minutes without oxygen before it is irreversibly damaged, so a delay in resuscitation may mean that, although a life is saved, the person can be seriously damaged mentally – in short, a vegetable for the rest of his life.

Mouth-to-mouth ventilation

(1) Remove any obstruction in the mouth and lay the child on his back. A small child can be held in the air by the legs to quickly let water or vomit drain from the mouth and lungs.
(2) Place one hand under the neck, the other on the forehead and tilt the head

back. Then move the hand which was under the neck to the chin and push the chin up in order to lift the tongue clear of the airway.

(3) Take a breath. For a small child, cover both the nose and mouth with your mouth and puff very gently. For an older child, pinch his nostrils, put your lips around his mouth and blow. In both cases pay careful attention to the chest rising.

As adults' lungs are much stronger and bigger than a child's, one must be extremely careful not to over-inflate and so damage the lungs. This depends on the size of the child, and is why it is essential to keep an eye on the chest as one blows gently.

(4) When the chest has risen fully, move your mouth away and finish breathing out.

(5) After the child's chest has fallen, repeat the process, but give the first few breaths in quick succession before the chest falls completely.

(6) Now check the carotid pulse in the hollow of the neck near the voice box – it is more reliable than the wrist pulse to ascertain if the heart is still beating.

(7) If the heart is beating, continue to give mouth-to-mouth ventilation until the child is breathing normally. It may be necessary to give partial help as the breathing recovers in gasps and starts. Keep an eye on the child's breathing for several hours afterwards.

(8) If the heart is not beating, begin chest compression. Children need less pressure than an adult, so place only one hand over the centre of the breastbone, press down about an inch (2.5 cm) and release, doing about fifteen compressions in about ten seconds. Then give a couple more mouth-to-mouth and nose ventilations.

For babies, use only two fingers over the centre of the breastbone and press less hard, about half an inch (1.5 cm).

Two people can work together effectively, one person doing the breathing while the other does the chest compression at the rate of 100 compressions and 20 breaths a minute; that is, approximately five compressions to each inflation of the lungs.

(9) Check the pulse every minute.

It is difficult to say how long one should continue if the child does not revive. There have been a few instances of children being successfully revived after several hours of resuscitation.

Once breathing has been restarted, other problems can be dealt with, although major bleeding can be stopped by a second person while mouth-to-mouth ventilation is going on. Bleeding can usually be stopped quite easily by firm direct pressure on the bleeding point with fingers or the palm of the hand. Even major bleeding can be halted this way. Pressure should be kept on the wound for five to fifteen minutes in order to give the blood time to clot.

Burns

Burns are a hazard on a moving boat, even if one is careful to keep children away from the stove and the pouring of hot liquids. During six years of living on board, a burn was the only serious accident we had, when Ivan tipped a bowl of hot custard down his bare chest. Being a thick viscous mixture, it stuck to his skin excruciatingly. Fortunately I knew what to do and, although a sizeable patch of skin was completely burnt off, not even a scar remains today.

The first thing to do with a burn is to immediately cool the affected skin area to prevent further or deeper damage. This can be done by plunging a hand or foot in a bowl of clean cold water (iced if possible) or by standing under a cold shower for ten minutes. Even cooling the area with buckets of clean sea water will do if this is more readily available than fresh water. The most important thing is to cool the skin. Once that is done time can be taken over further treatment.

If the burn is at all serious, there are two dangers: infection and the loss of fluid leading to shock. The entire burn area should therefore be thoroughly disinfected. Wash your hands and any instruments such as scissors in a disinfectant solution. Swab the skin area carefully with disinfectant and then

A few days after being burnt on the chest, Ivan sports a burn dressing held carefully in place, while assembling his train set on the aft deck for an audience in the Solomon Islands.

49

cover with a special sterile burn dressing. If the burn covers a large area, it may not be possible to cover this with a burn dressing, so place the child on a clean sheet and leave the burn open to the air after swabbing, making a tent over the child with another sheet so that no material comes in contact with the burn. If the burn is severe, start a course of antibiotic to prevent infection.

For the second danger of shock and fluid loss, give the child plenty of his favourite drink in small but frequent sips, for example several cups an hour, especially during the first hour.

Medical assistance should be sought urgently for any major burn, and if anything over 20 per cent of the body surface is affected it should be considered as a burn that can have lethal consequences if not properly treated.

I have dealt with the major emergencies first, because immediate first aid is of such importance. There are many other things which are equally important or serious, but they can usually be dealt with in a more leisurely manner.

Protection from disease

It is important to check that one's child has had all necessary vaccinations before leaving on a cruise. Children are normally immunised in infancy against various diseases, such as diphtheria, tetanus, whooping cough and poliomyelitis, and booster doses given at around five years of age. Immunisation against tetanus is highly recommended for anyone, child or adult, who is planning to sail extensively. Tetanus is a very unpleasant disease, with a high mortality rate, and any wound, such as could be inflicted by a rusty nail protruding from a dock, carries the risk of infection by tetanus. A booster dose of tetanus toxoid should be given every five years.

Poliomyelitis is much more common in other parts of the world than in the developed countries, and this is another vaccine normally given in infancy, with booster doses at intervals, which should not be neglected. Smallpox vaccination is now not necessary as smallpox has been virtually eradicated worldwide. Other vaccinations may be recommended for certain areas, depending on which countries one is cruising to, and local health offices will advise on this. In many countries there are regularly cases of enteric fever (typhoid and paratyphoid), so that the TAB vaccination is a sensible precaution for anyone sailing extensively abroad.

Malaria

There has been an upsurge of the malarial parasite worldwide and it is an increasing health problem affecting many pleasant cruising areas, such as the

Solomon Islands and Papua New Guinea. It is also endemic in many parts of central and southern America, Africa and South-East Asia. Malaria takes a particularly heavy toll on children and so prophylactic tablets should be taken all the time one cruises in a malarial area. Again local health offices will be able to give up-to-date information on which areas are affected.

The usual prophylactic drug is chloroquine taken weekly, the dosage being one eighth of the adult dose for infants under one year, one quarter for those one to four years old, one half for the four to eight year olds, three quarters for the eight to twelves, while those over twelve can take the adult dose. There is a chloroquine syrup available, which may be easier to give to small children than tablets. Some antimalarials such as pyrimethamine are not recommended for the under fives. Amodiaquine, which previously had been formulated for infants, has since been discovered to have the serious side effect of affecting white blood cells in some people, sometimes fatal. Mefloquine, a new drug, may be effective in chloroquine resistant areas. Initial testing on 100,000 patients in Thailand suggest mefloquine may be safe for children and pregnant women.

The upsurge in malaria is partly due to an increased resistance of the parasite to drugs such as chloroquine, and advice should be sought in a particular area about this resistance and which prophylactic drug is recommended. Up to date advice can be obtained from immunisation centres or public health offices, eg British Airways Travel Centres, PPP Medical Centre, 99 New Cavendish St, London W1 or MASTA, a medical advisory service for travellers, run from the London School of Hygiene and Tropical Medicine, Keppel St, London WC1E 7HT. A fee is charged for this service.

There is a lot to be said for mosquito netting, against not only malarial mosquitos, but also other insects. These insects rarely fly far from the shore, so it is when anchored close by the shore or tied to a dock that they can present a problem. One of the worst places we were afflicted was in the enclosed sounds and rivers of North Carolina, while sailing along the Intracoastal waterway. Detachable frames with mosquito netting can be made to fit over hatches or alternatively netting can be rigged up over a child's bunk – a much better solution where babies and small children are concerned than smothering their sensitive skins with insect repellent. Prevention of the bite is easier than trying to keep a child from scratching, with attendant risk of infection.

Medical chest

A basic first aid kit should be mandatory on any boat and there are plenty of commercial kits on the market to choose from. For a longer cruise a more comprehensive selection of medicines than those contained in most kits will be necessary in order to deal with a wide range of possible illnesses and injuries away from professional help.

The following is a recommended list for an offshore cruise, in respect of children; it does not include drugs for adults. Those items marked with an asterisk are only available on prescription in most countries. Some of the items will be discussed in more detail later in the chapter.

Cotton wool
Waterproof adhesive dressings in a variety of sizes
Sterilised gauze
Bandages and surgical tape
Crepe bandages for sprains
Sterile packs of dressings specially prepared for burns
Scissors, forceps, safety pins, thermometer
Disposable syringes and needles
Sterile needles with sutures for stitching a wound
General disinfectant (Dettol, pHisohex, Cetavlon)
Antiseptic cream or solution (Savlon, Cetavlex, T.C.P.)
Calomine lotion to soothe sunburn or insect bites
Promethazine cream for the prevention of infection in minor burns and insect
     bites (Phenergan)
Promethazine elixir as a sedative and hypnotic as well as for allergies to food,
     insect bites, jellyfish stings (Phenergan)
*Antibiotic cream or powder (achromycin or neomycin)
*Antibiotic tablets or paediatric suspension (ampicillin,amoxycillin)
Laxative
Antidiarrhoeal
Analgesic (painkiller such as paracetamol)
*Local anaesthetic for stitching or cleaning a major wound
*Ear and eye drops (framycetin)
Antifungal preparations for athlete's foot and other fungal infections
Piperazine sachets for threadworm and roundworm (Pripsen)
Shampoo for head lice (malathion or carbaryl)
Antiseasickness tablets
Antimalarial tablets or syrup (chloroquine)
Sun-screen cream

To this list add any special medicine that your child may need, such as for asthma or eczema.

As a general principle, the dosage of a medicine for a child can be calculated on his body weight as a proportion of an average adult weight. However, certain drugs used by adults are not recommended for small children, so attention should be paid to the manufacturer's accompanying instructions. Medicines in liquid or syrup form are much preferred by children and paediatric formulations should be bought for the medicine chest wherever possible.

With my pharmacist's training, I organised the medical locker on *Aventura* extremely carefully. Inside each bottle of tablets I put a note giving the name of the drug, its use and dosage, just in case the labels came off (which they never did) but also in case someone else apart from me had to play doctor. The bottles were packed in watertight boxes, in fact empty icecream containers of a hard plastic. All the non-urgent items were put at the back of the locker and the commonly used ones, such as antiseptic, near the front. Items that might be required urgently were also kept near the front, organised into different coloured plastic bags. One contained everything needed for burns, while another held all that was needed to treat a serious cut or wound. The disposable syringes and needles were carried because these are not available in many countries and hepatitis is a real risk from improperly sterilised needles. When we needed to be immunised against cholera after an outbreak in Tarawa in Kiribati (the Gilbert Islands), we took along our own needles and syringes.

Needless to say, if small children are on board, the medical locker should preferably be out of easy reach and also kept locked.

The potency of most medicines decreases with age and this is accelerated by the poor storage conditions that prevail on most boats and especially in humid tropical conditions. Potent drugs such as antibiotics should be renewed every couple of years, and drugs usually have an expiry date printed on the packaging. Drugs can be used after the expiry date if nothing else is available, but probably they will be less effective and the dosage may have to be increased. For those drugs for which a prescription is required, most family doctors are quite willing to oblige if the reasons are fully explained. Many doctors will also advise anyone setting off on an ocean passage which drugs are suitable for children's use.

Whenever a child is ill, it is advisable to try to obtain medical advice as soon as possible. The radio, whether VHF, marine or amateur, is usually the best way to achieve this, requesting *medico service*. Normally this will result in the caller being connected to the casualty department of the nearest hospital. Amateur radio is becoming increasingly popular on yachts and is ideal when cruising out of VHF range. Many of the amateur maritime networks based in various parts of the world, as for example Hawaii or California, have medical specialists on 24 hour call. The usual procedure is to describe the symptoms and what drugs are available in the boat's medicine chest. The doctor then can advise a suitable course of treatment over the radio. For urgent medical advice or assistance, the correct signal is MEDICO followed by PAN-PAN repeated three times.

Part of the problem when one is away from home base is to know when a symptom is serious enough to seek advice. The following list may provide a guideline for an anxious parent.

Symptoms for which medical advice should be sought

- Acute abdominal pain with vomiting
- Vomiting blood
- Head injury followed by vomiting, drowsiness or a fit
- A convulsion or fit of any kind
- Progressive drowsiness especially with a raised temperature
- A cough associated with rapid breathing and pain
- Headache at the back of the head
- Stiffness of the neck in a sick child
- Earache or suspected hearing difficulties
- Loss of weight

As well as common minor ailments which are not serious enough to seek outside help, situations may arise where medical advice is difficult to obtain or maybe a radio is not available. Some of these common complaints and their treatment will be examined in the following pages.

Seasickness

Small babies rarely appear to suffer from seasickness and this condition usually only appears after the age of six months. A lot of children who have grown up on boats are never afflicted, while a few suffer quite badly and others are seasick to varying degrees. Although the reasons why some people are more afflicted than others is not known, psychological factors can make seasickness worse – especially the behaviour of over-anxious parents.

When talking to long distance voyagers for a survey, I found that about half of the children suffered from seasickness to a greater or lesser degree, especially for the first few days after a lengthy stay in port. None of these parents gave any medication to their children, not even to children who suffered more severely. The usual remedy for seasick children was to encourage them to lie down in their bunks with a favourite toy or a good book. It is also important to keep the children from being bored or cold. Fortunately children do not have to deal with boathandling or watchkeeping, so it does not matter if they are lying down or drowsy a lot of the time.

An empty stomach sends a similar signal to the brain as the feeling of being sick, so it is important not to let the stomach get empty too often. One way to prevent this is to give a child small snacks at regular intervals between meals, such as a banana, some crackers or biscuits. This keeps a sense of fullness in the stomach.

Children have a marvellous natural resilience and often will adapt to adverse conditions more readily than an adult. Unlike adults they are less likely to feel ashamed or worried about the physical act of vomiting, especially if the parents make little fuss about it. In my experience it is most likely that ten minutes later they will be wanting something to eat. My own children were occasionally sick in heavy weather especially after a long stay in port, but I cannot ever remember them missing a meal.

It always surprised me what violent motion the children were able to sleep through, although their normal cabin was the fo'c'sle, which is the least comfortable part in rough weather. Often when it was rough they slept elsewhere, the cockpit cushions on the main cabin floor being the favourite place. It was better to have to step over a happy sleeping body than to have a miserable seasick child conveniently out of the way.

Many of the drugs which are most effective against seasickness, such as cinnarizine (Stugeron) or promethazine (Avomine), are not recommended for children under five. Those over five can take half of the adult dose. Children under five could take a quarter of a tablet of dimenhydrate (Dramamine), the six to twelve year old dose is half a tablet and the over twelves can take the adult dose. This drug is not recommended for infants under one year old. Personally I would hesitate before giving any drugs to a child for seasickness, only doing so if the child is in real distress about the condition, or maybe if an older teenage child is seasick.

Stomach upsets

Changes in the normal routine, different foods and drinks can all help to give an upset stomach, either diarrhoea or constipation, the latter being a common complaint on boats.

Many of the stronger antidiarrhoeal preparations are not recommended for children and cannot be bought without a prescription. An effective solution for a child is to give a large spoonful of a simple kaolin suspension, which any chemist will make up without a prescription. This will usually settle most minor diarrhoea. Children over five years can be given a kaolin mixture with added codeine.

If the diarrhoea is severe or continuous, it may be necessary to give something stronger, but it is very important to check the correct dosage and give only a drug that is recommended for children. For example, one tablet of Lomotil (diphenoxylate hydrochloride with atropine sulphate) can be given twice a day from one to three years old, three times a day for four to eight year olds, and four times a day for nine to twelve year olds. Older children can be given two tablets three times a day. Lomotil is also available in liquid form where one 5 ml spoonful is equivalent to a tablet. An alternative drug to use in cases of bacterial diarrhoea or gastro-enteritis is Ivax (neomycin sulphate in a kaolin suspension), where one to five year olds can be given 5 ml (one teaspoonful) four times daily and older children 15 ml (that is, three teaspoonfuls) four times daily. A prescription is needed for both drugs and they should be used with caution.

If one is cruising with a baby under one year old, one of the reasons for recommending breastfeeding for a more prolonged period than on dry land is that this does lessen the risk of diarrhoea in the baby.

One of the dangers in continuing diarrhoea is dehydration and the fluid intake of the child should be kept up. If a child has trouble in keeping fluid down, it is worth trying a thin purée of potatoes, which lines the stomach wall. An excellent replacement fluid if available is the fresh juice from the young green coconut. This has the right balance of essential salts and straight from the nut the added advantage of being sterile. Children do become dehydrated much more rapidly than adults, and so whenever diarrhoea or vomiting persists, for whatever reason, the child should be encouraged to sip sweetened water.

The opposite problem of constipation is often met with while cruising, sometimes because of changed diet or reduced consumption of fresh fruit and vegetables. Older children who start sailing for the first time may feel inhibited about using the head or making a smell or noise when in the confines of a boat. Reassurance and a no-fuss attitude by parents should overcome this.

The first solution to the problem of constipation is to increase the child's intake of water, fruit and bran cereals. Try and encourage the child to go to the head as soon as he feels the urge, not to ignore Nature's call, as some children are prone to do if they are absorbed in a game or lying in their bunks. A mild laxative, such as syrup of figs, can be given to help the emptying of the bowel, but should be stopped as soon as possible. Laxatives can be harmful as they may irritate the bowel and can help constipation to turn into a chronic problem as well as starting the habit of relying on a drug. They should only be given if there is pain or bleeding associated with really hard stools.

Bed-wetting is another problem that may distress a child or cause him to be concerned about a weekend sailing trip. A surprising number of healthy children take several years to achieve full control over their bladders and this applies more to boys than girls. Mainly it is due to a delay in the maturation of the relevant part of the central nervous system. Psychological factors can make it worse, for example if the child is insecure or worried about finding his way to the head in the dark or while the boat is in motion.

It is unreasonable to blame a child for something he does in his sleep, so the most important treatment is to reassure the child and reduce his feelings of anxiety about it. Punishment of any kind, even verbal admonition, is likely to do harm and delay control. Cutting out drinks for a couple of hours before bedtime and making sure the child empties his bladder before turning in can help. Also a dim light can be left on, if apprehension about getting up in the dark appears to be one of the causes. Over the years scores of drugs have been tried for this common childhood problem, but with little agreement among the medical profession as to their success. If bed-wetting persists in children over five, the most successful treatment appears to be a special pad, which the child wears and which activates an electric buzzer to wake him as soon as the first few drops of urine touch the pad.

Sunburn and heat illness

The effect of the sun is stronger at sea, partly because the air may be less polluted which, combined with the reflective property of water, intensifies ultra-violet rays. Also one may often be less aware of the sun's strength due to wind and breezes blowing over the skin. For these reasons the amount of exposure to sun that a child is getting should be carefully monitored until a protective tan has developed. Very blond and red haired children tend to burn much more easily and need a protective sun-filter cream, although this should be applied warily to sensitive skins, checking that no allergy develops. Covering the child with long sleeved cotton clothing such as loose pyjamas may be a better solution, while babies and infants particularly should always wear a sun hat. A few children never develop enough tan to protect their skin and will always have to be protected from the sun in some way or another; but, for the majority, once a healthy tan is established the need for sunscreen preparations can be reduced. It has now been established that excessive exposure to the sun and burning of the skin as a child increases the probability of the eventual formation of skin cancer. This is a particular risk for those with fair skins who burn easily. The protection of all children from sunburn is therefore of prime importance. If sunburn does occur, it is treated as any other burn and in severe cases an antihistamine cream such as promethazine can be used to prevent infection.

When sailing one moves much more slowly into a new environment compared to many other methods of travel, and so a certain adaptation to a hotter climate takes place gradually. Heat illness, either as heat exhaustion or a heatstroke, can occur, although this is most likely to affect those who are unacclimatised, as when flying in to charter or visit friends. In certain areas where the temperature is extremely high, for example in the Red Sea, heat illness is a risk for all members of the crew.

The symptoms are a listlessness accompanied by headache and nausea. The pulse is usually rapid and the skin feels clammy. Sometimes a prickly heat rash can develop. These symptoms can progress to a heatstroke, when sweating stops, leaving the skin dry and burning. Collapse into unconsciousness can occur in this case, but the most dramatic effect is the sudden rise in body temperature.

The most urgent action is to cool the child and reduce the body temperature. Strip the child naked, put him in the coolest place and sponge with cold water, iced if possible. Directing a small fan onto the skin will also help. The next priority is to replace the fluid and salt loss, by drinking water or lemonade to which salt has been added in the proportion of one teaspoon to one pint (5 ml to half a litre). As this is not very palatable, it should be taken in small sips to prevent vomiting.

In very hot climates a good preventive measure is to drink more than usual and increase one's salt intake by adding more salt to meals or by taking salt tablets. Meals should be light when eaten in the middle of the day, and exposure to the midday sun reduced. If a child does become listless, it is wise to step up his salt and water intake immediately.

Skin infections

Nearly every long distance cruising family I have come across in tropical climates has had at one time or another trouble with infected cuts or insect bites, which can turn into tropical ulcers at alarming speed in some areas. Eventually I learnt to painstakingly disinfect and treat every minute scratch, graze or insect bite, that normally we would not have worried about.

At the first sign of any infection the cut should be treated with an antibiotic cream or powder containing neomycin or tetracycline, or alternatively a sulphonamide powder. Powders can be more effective than creams under the moist tropical conditions that bacteria thrive in, because the cut is kept drier. I found that all treatments became less effective as the years we spent sailing in the tropics increased, presumably because we were lowering our resistance, which was only solved by a return to a temperate climate. Neomycin aerosol sprays can cause the side effect of deafness if used on damaged skin on any part of the body and are not recommended in the treatment of infected cuts.

These recurring infections are usually due to a staphylococcus infection, a common affliction among those cruising in the tropics, and this has to be treated by an internal course of an antibiotic to eliminate the bacteria from the bloodstream. The importance of treating all minor cuts and grazes seriously while sailing in warm climates cannot be emphasised too strongly.

Not only bacteria, but other organisms also, love damp conditions and fungal infections such as athlete's foot are much more common afloat than ashore. As children are so often barefoot and in wet conditions, the feet stay damp and are therefore prone to catch this condition of cracked broken skin that itches and can become very red and raw. Drying the feet well and keeping them exposed to air helps prevent the infection, sandals being preferable to socks and shoes. Dusting the infected area with a powder such as zinc undecenoate (Tineafax) or tolfanate (Tineaderm) is effective.

Nits and worms

Children seem to have a talent for picking up certain things that adults rarely do, such as threadworms or head lice, especially when they are travelling. The first sign of the latter is usually the nits or eggs that stick to individual hairs and an infestation of this sort is easily cured in a few days by shampooing with a specific shampoo containing carbaryl or malathion.

Threadworms can be equally effectively dispatched with piperazine, usually sold as a raspberry flavoured powder which is made up into a drink. Dosage is according to age: one third of a sachet from three months to one year old, two thirds of a sachet for the one to six year olds, while over six a whole sachet can be given. Threadworms are not serious and only annoying because of the itching around the anus at night. If children never ate with their fingers or put their fingers in their mouths without first washing them, then the infection would be eliminated. Unfortunately few small children can be relied on not to do this. If the infection does recur, it might be worth dosing the whole crew.

Swimmer's ear and ear infections

When children are in and out of the water continually, especially if they dive or go underwater a lot, they are very susceptible to ear infections. One way to prevent this is to make sure they dry their ears effectively with cotton wool when they come out of the water. There is also a drying solution containing glycerol which aids drying and a drop is added to each ear after swimming.

If at all possible, medical advice should be sought in all cases of ear infection or earache. This is to check that the ear drum is not perforated, because there is a risk of permanent damage and deafness if some antibiotic ear drops, such as framycetin, are used when the ear drum is perforated. Infections of the external ear can be cured by these drops, but for otitis of the middle ear an internally administered antibiotic may be necessary. Some of the antibiotic ear drops are also formulated as eye drops, so they can be used in bacterial infections of the eye, styes and conjunctivitis.

Serious infections

Nearly all serious infections are likely to require antibiotic treatment and these are drugs which must not be used indiscriminately or treated lightly. Medical advice should be sought either ashore locally or over the radio as to their use and dosage for a child. However, if one does not have a long range radio, or one is in a remote area or on an ocean passage, it may be essential to begin treatment quickly and a decision will have to be taken on a course of treatment.

If an ocean passage is to be included in the cruising plans, it is worthwhile discussing with one's doctor which drugs would be most suitable for a child, especially as a prescription will be required. Many antibiotics are available as syrups or paediatric suspensions, which are easier to give a child than a tablet. It is also a good idea to stock more than one antibiotic in the medicine chest, as different antibiotics are effective against different ranges of bacteria. Some people have a sensitivity to penicillin and if possible try to discover whether this is the case beforehand.

Ampicillin is one penicillin derivative which is effective against a wide range of infections and can be bought both as a syrup and a powder which makes up into a solution, especially formulated for children. The powder is in a sealed bottle and, when required for use, distilled water is added and the bottle shaken. If distilled water is not available, ordinary water should be boiled and left to cool before making up the solution. Some other antibiotics which are available in suspensions suitable for children are amoxycillin, effective in respiratory, genito-urinary tract and ear, nose and throat infections, and Septrin (trimethoprim and sulphamethoxazole) which can be used by those sensitive to penicillin. Tetracycline is an antibiotic in common use, which is effective against a wide spectrum of bacteria, but it should *never* be used for children under twelve years of age. The full course of an antibiotic should always be followed, even after symptoms have subsided, and any solution left over should be discarded as it does not keep once it is made up.

Treatment with antibiotics can be quite dramatic in its success, as one example might illustrate. Sailing in the Caribbean, we spent several days anchored off Saline island, an uninhabited island north of Grenada and close to Carriacou. One evening my daughter Doina, then nine years old, felt slightly unwell and was running a temperature. I wondered if she might have a slight intoxication from fish, as freshly caught fish figured largely in our diet. The next morning, however, her temperature had risen alarmingly to 40°C (104°C) and I began to get worried. There seemed no real reason for her high temperature nor any other symptoms, but on inspection her throat and tonsils did look slightly red and swollen. Immediately I started giving her a course of ampicillin and also a rub down with cold water. The response to the antibiotic was quick and in 24 hours she was back to normal, although I did continue the treatment for another two days to be sure the infection was controlled.

An attack of appendicitis is something that many parents fear and is one of the most likely reasons for acute abdominal pain in children and young people. Antibiotics can suppress appendicitis until port is reached, although an operation may still be necessary. This is one good reason for carrying antibiotics in the medical chest while cruising. In fact, if a child complains of abdominal pain, it might well be only a stomach upset due to something eaten or because of constipation or diarrhoea, but it does no harm to check for appendicitis. The following symptoms provide a guideline.

(1) A vague central pain, which settles into a sharp pain in the lower right abdomen. There will be tenderness in this area when touched.

(2) The child usually vomits once or twice after the pain begins.

(3) Maybe there is one loose evacuation of the bowels at first, but then constipation sets in.

(4) A rising temperature and a steadily rising pulse rate occur. A rising pulse rate, which can go up every hour, is the surest sign that treatment is urgent.

If appendicitis is suspected, firstly give no solid food of any kind at all, just sips of plain water to relieve thirst. Secondly, begin a course of ampicillin or penicillin. Do *not* give a laxative for the constipation as any irritation to the intestines can increase the chance of the appendix rupturing. Make the child comfortable, propped up in his bunk; heat applied to the painful area with a covered hot water bottle can relieve the pain. An analgesic can be given (suitable painkillers for children are discussed in the next section).

The pulse should be taken every two hours and the temperature every six hours. The first sign that recovery is taking place is that the pulse rate begins to slow back down to normal. A child's pulse rate is usually higher than an adult's, especially babies and infants, being about ten beats a minute less when the child is asleep. (As the range of normal pulse rates is large, it might be worthwhile noting a child's normal pulse rate while in good health.) Other signs of recovery are a decrease in the pain, the temperature returning to normal and the cessation of any vomiting. Nevertheless appendicitis can easily flare up again, so the child should be kept on a light diet and resting until port is reached and a doctor can be consulted.

Treating a child's pain

If a child is in pain, from a bad wound, fracture, serious injury or for some other reason such as appendicitis, he cannot be given the same painkillers as adults. Most strong analgesics are not recommended for children, mainly because an overdose can have serious consequences. A suitable analgesic for children would be an elixir of paracetamol. Although not recommended for those under three months, babies over that age and up to one year can be given a 5 ml dose (one teaspoonful) four times a day. One to five year olds can take 10 ml (two teaspoonfuls) four times a day and the over fives the adult dose of up to 20 ml (four teaspoonfuls) four times a day. Paracetamol is also an antipyretic and so will act to bring down the temperature of a sick child as well.

For very severe pain as might result from a major accident pentazocine could be used, either in the form of capsules or as an injection. Over one year of age, the dose of the injection is calculated on the body weight of the child. The capsules are only recommended for over six year olds and all these pentazocine preparations need a prescription. They should never be used if there is a head injury.

A better solution for a sick child than giving painkillers is to give a sedative, such as promethazine (Phenergan elixir). This can be given to small children from six months old and also has a hypnotic action which will help a sick child to sleep. This elixir is very useful to have on board as it also has an antihistaminic action against allergies and can be used if a child gets an allergic reaction to food, insect bites or jellyfish stings.

A healthy diet

Ensuring a balanced and healthy diet will increase a child's chances both of successfully resisting infection and of combating disease or injury should it occur. It is not too difficult to keep a good supply of fresh food on a boat if items are properly stored. Fruits such as apples, oranges and grapefruits store well, either

After a torrential downpour in Panama, Ivan and Doina enjoy a bath in the water collected in the dinghy.

individually wrapped in newspaper or suspended in net bags. Potatoes, onions, carrots and hard salad cabbages are some vegetables that can be stored for a considerable time, the two latter being of higher nutritional value if eaten raw. The secret is in the shopping, and all fruits and vegetables should be hand picked and chosen for their quality prior to a passage. A stem of bananas hanging in the rigging is a trademark of boats sailing in the tropics and the fruits can be picked off the stem as they ripen. Carefully selected green tomatoes slowly ripened on our passage across the Atlantic, lasting almost to the final day. At no time in our circumnavigation were we completely without some fresh produce, even if it was sometimes unusual, such as green pumpkin tips or unripe green papaya, which can be grated and mixed with a salad dressing.

A growing child does need plenty of protein and often in places where fresh meat is difficult to find fresh fish can be caught or bought instead. Smoked and processed cheeses are another source of protein that have a long storage life and the dried pulses, such as beans, peas and lentils, should not be ignored. If eggs are fresh they usually keep for six weeks without any further treatment.

The easiest course of action if one is in any doubt about diet while cruising is to take a daily supplement of multivitamins, a procedure that can do no harm. As the body does not store some of these vitamins, it is more important to have a daily intake of a smaller quantity than a larger amount all at once, a principle which also applies to fresh fruit.

In interviewing over a hundred long distance voyagers at various times in the Pacific, some twenty-five of whom had children with them, and from my own experiences during a six year long circumnavigation, I have drawn the conclusion that children on boats are a distinctly healthy lot. I have not come across any cases of appendicitis nor any of the childhood infections such as measles or mumps. The only serious medical problems reported to me were two cases of viral infections of unknown origin, one of which resulted in severe dehydration of the small child and necessitated a speedy transfer to a local hospital. In general, children seemed more resistant than adults and the constantly changing atmosphere that cruising brings had helped them build up a healthy resistance to many diseases and infections.

Books

The Ship Captain's Medical Guide. London: HMSO.
The Essentials of First Aid. (1983) London: The Order of St John.
Counter, R. T. (1985) *The Yachtsman's Doctor*. London: Nautical Books.
Eastman, P. (1987) *Advanced First Aid Afloat*. 3rd Edition. International Marine.

6
Babies and Infants

A gently rocking boat is an ideal cradle for a sleeping baby and the very young are usually quite content in a watery environment. Until their mobility and desire to be entertained increases, small babies create few problems if they are kept fed, clean and secure. Without the conveniences of a modern home, achieving this requires a certain amount of organisation, but fortunately there are many products on the market designed for travelling with small children, whether by land, sea or air, which help make life easier for the parent of today.

First and foremost in requirements is a snug and secure place for the baby, which he cannot fall out of in a seaway. As berths on a boat are normally adult size, this is best achieved by putting a small baby to sleep in a basket or carrycot, usually with handles on it so it can also be used for transporting the child. The cot must be wedged firmly into the bunk so it cannot slide about, which can be done easily with cushions or pillows. If the weather is rough, the baby himself might need to be stopped from rolling in some way, such as with a folded-up blanket or towel tucked along his side. If a basket or carrycot is not used, the baby must be wedged firmly in the bunk so that there is no danger of suffocation should he roll to one side. Only at about five to six months old will a baby be able to roll over from his front onto his back or vice versa on his own.

There are various types of travelling and folding cots on the market, even some that convert to baby seats or adapt into a pushchair as well. The choice will depend on how much space is available and whether the cot or basket has to serve elsewhere apart from on the boat. A cot of plastic material has many advantages in a salty atmosphere; it is easier to keep clean and will not become damp as some natural fibres do in moist conditions. The natural fibres of a basket, however,

Brigitte Sperka and Frances Stocks on board *Aventura* in Bali. Both their six month old daughters already had hundreds of miles of sailing behind them.

are much pleasanter to the touch than plastic. A softer basket may be easier to store out of the way when not in use, yet a cot with rigid sides can be wedged more easily into a bunk, the sides of the cot providing extra protection for the baby.

The bunk should have a leeboard or leecloth high enough to contain whatever the baby is sleeping in. Netting can be fixed from the board or cloth to completely enclose the bunk, so that in no circumstances will the baby fall out. This netting should be fastened with hooks or studs so that it can be opened easily when required.

A carrycot is a bulky item to store on a boat, and once a baby can sit and crawl a basket or cot can be discarded if space is at a premium. Even so, all small children must be tucked into snug berths that they cannot easily fall out of and sandwiched with cushions or pillows to stop them moving about too much. Equally one must be sure that nothing can fall onto them from nearby shelves or other berths. One solution is a high leecloth that can be clipped up at night and let down in the day. This cloth should be reinforced and strengthened so it will stand up to the daily wear and tear that is normal with an active child. An alternative to a leecloth is a wooden board which can be slotted in at the edge of a bunk, but a permanent arrangement of built-in higher sides to a child's bunk might be worth considering. This is only possible if the berth is not also used as a day settee. If the children have a separate cabin or the forepeak berths this can be arranged more easily. On our boat the wooden sides to the children's berths in the forward cabin were built much higher at the head end of their bunks, although these sides tapered away towards the foot.

Out of the way

Netting which encloses the entire bunk and can be fastened up to the ceiling from the outside can be used with older active infants too, not just to keep them safe while asleep, but also while they are playing. This playpen arrangement not only stops the child getting out, but at the same time allows him to see what is happening in the rest of the boat, where his parents are and what they are doing.

Most of the points made in the earlier chapter on safety afloat apply particularly to babies and infants. A crawler or toddler on a boat requires almost constant supervision and can rarely be left to his own devices without some watch being kept over him. It is not only that toddlers can hurt themselves or fall overboard, but they can also easily cause trouble by twiddling the dials or moving settings on radios, autopilots or Satnavs. It is difficult for a small child to understand that these things are not to be touched, especially instruments that have digital readouts blinking so attractively. Keeping radio contact with the Canadian yacht *Kleena Kleene II* as we sailed at the same time across the Indian Ocean and up the Red Sea, Bill Stocks was late for our schedule several times because his one year old daughter had detuned the radio. In an emergency such a mishap could be crucial.

Some method of keeping an infant out of the way has to be considered, such as a netted-over bunk, which can only be opened from the outside by an adult. In an emergency situation, when both parents may be needed on deck, a way of quickly immobilising a small child safely must be found. While a netted-over bunk is one solution, another is to strap the child into a seat similar to those used in cars and from which he cannot undo himself. A car seat itself could easily be adapted to fit over a settee berth, being firmly attached to anchoring points as in a car. These seats are easily removed when required, leaving only the anchoring points and webbing attached.

In such circumstances, give the child some of his favourite toys and, if he still objects, ignore him and get on quickly with the task in hand. A few minutes' crying will not do a small child any harm – not as much as leaving him unrestrained and unwatched, or neglecting a vital job in the sailing of the boat. As children grow up, they will soon come to realise that in certain situations the handling of the boat takes precedence over anything else and that parents are best not bothered in these circumstances. The safety of the boat must always come first.

Feeding baby

The old adage that mother's milk is best is nowhere truer than on a boat, and in fact most sailing mothers I have met have carried on breastfeeding their babies much longer than they probably would have done living on land. This does avoid the need for sterilising bottles and the extra storage space required for the equipment involved in bottle feeding. However, a few mothers choose to bottle feed so that the father can also be involved in feeding the baby, especially sharing the night feeds, and this does have a certain advantage, particularly on an ocean passage. If a baby is being bottle fed, the bottles and teats can be sterilised by leaving them in a sterilising solution in a container with a tight fitting lid, proper sealing of this unit being vitally important on a moving boat. As infant formula has to be made up with boiled water to avoid infection, it is more convenient to make up a whole day's supply at once, but this can only be done if there is a refrigerator on the boat to store the bottles in, or alternatively an insulated container with ice or frozen icebags. Infant formula should never be kept warm for any length of time in a thermos flask or stored in warm conditions, because this encourages the growth of bacteria. All feeding equipment should be sterilised until babies are at least four months old. In warm climates the formula will have to be made up as required if one has no refrigeration, keeping the opened packet in as cool a place as possible.

Apart from the performance of sterilising bottles and making up formula, one reason sailing mothers breastfeed longer, often even after their babies are old enough to drink from a cup, is that breastfeeding greatly reduces the risk of stomach upsets and diarrhoea, particularly important when cruising away from home in foreign waters. In some developing countries infant formula is not available except on prescription, a measure which has been introduced to encourage women to breastfeed in these countries and so reduce infant mortality and illness due to inadequate sterilisation of infant formula mix.

Fresh milk is rarely available in the tropics, although the advent of UHT (long life) milk has greatly improved matters for sailing families. Although closer to the real thing than powdered milk, UHT milk does not quite have the same taste as fresh milk, and cold fresh milk was one of my children's delights when we arrived in countries like New Zealand and Australia. Carrying powdered milk in the ship's stores does not save weight because one has to carry the extra water needed to make it up. The cartons of UHT milk are thus one way of conserving fresh water supplies and an important standby if water is in short supply or is polluted. Fruit juices are now also available treated in this way to increase their storage life.

Breastfeeding can be very tiring, especially in the early weeks when more night feeds are given, and this tiredness can reduce the flow of milk. If possible a nursing mother should not have to do night watches at all. Many parents avoid longer passages until their baby sleeps through the night or else take on extra crew for the passage. After the birth of their son Tristan in Suva, Ian and Derry Hancock took someone with them to help sail their 30 foot *Runestaff* on the passage from Fiji to New Zealand, although they did not normally take on crew. Any delay in their departure would have meant staying on into the hurricane season in the South Pacific, which they were loathe to do with a small baby. Six week old Tristan sailed this 1,000 mile ocean passage without any problems.

For weaning a child, proprietary infant foods and cereals are now available in all major ports worldwide, but in remoter places the selection may be more limited or non-existent. However, many parents do prefer to give their child as much fresh food as possible and not rely on these convenience foods. Infant foods can easily be made from the fresh food of an adult meal, selecting small quantities of everything and grinding or sieving these to a mush suitable to be spooned to a baby. There are several small hand blenders or grinders on the market that achieve this, usually by rotation of the handle which turns grinding blades on a sieve. In most places, fresh fruit and vegetables are available even if it is only the ubiquitous banana, which is one of the easiest fruits to mash up for a baby. With milk and sugar it is a favourite of most small children. If in doubt about the adequacy of a diet for a child while cruising and the amount of fresh food available, extra vitamins can always be given. Spoonfuls of orange juice or rose hip syrup will provide vitamin C, and cod liver oil vitamins A and D. Even those parents who normally insist that their growing baby eats only fresh food can still be glad of being able to quickly open a tin or jar if the weather is bad or sailing conditions are tough. Babies rarely suffer from seasickness, but that does not mean that parents are also exempt, and so a quick solution to feeding baby is the answer in bad weather.

The other end!

The disposable nappy has made an enormous difference to cruising with a baby. For a weekend or short cruise disposables are the obvious choice, with one proviso: that one is careful where one disposes of them. Although marked as disposable and bio-degradable, the haphazard discarding of these items has polluted fringing reef and beaches. They should not be discarded overboard when in coastal waters, but should be collected into a tightly closed sealed bag and disposed of ashore on one's return. In mid-ocean, they should be shredded into smaller pieces before jettisoning.

Disposables are great for a weekend sail, but parents on a longer cruise often choose to use the terry towelling sort as well. Disposables are not always available in remote places and stocking up for a long period poses a problem as they are very bulky items to store. The amount needed for one small baby for several months would fill a whole bunk. They can also work out an expensive item for parents on a limited budget, especially if bought in countries where they are imported and not manufactured locally.

Many mothers cruising for longer periods of time use disposables for passages and terry cloth while in port where washing facilities and fresh water are more readily available. A limited water supply and the lack of a washing machine does make washing nappies an unwelcome chore on a sailing boat. However, it is not insurmountable, particularly if a sterilising powder (such as Napisan) is used. This powder is dissolved in cold water in a bucket with a lid; the nappies are then soaked in this solution overnight and only need to be rinsed out the following morning in fresh water. The thorough washing and rinsing is important in order to remove all the ammonia which results from the breakdown of urine. This is an irritant and easily causes a rash on a baby's sensitive skin. Frequent changing and careful drying of the baby's bottom can minimise the likelihood of a rash. In hot moist climates plastic pants will promote the formation of ammonia and also increase the chance of a heat rash, and so are best not used.

Water

Washing the nappies is just one of the ways that fresh water is consumed at an alarming rate when a baby is on board. As baby skin is sensitive, washing both skin and clothes in fresh water is necessary to prevent salt water sores or rashes. The amount of fresh water needed with a baby or infant on board is something that must be taken into consideration when planning for a cruise. If the water storage capacity of a boat is limited, extra fresh water can always be carried in jerrycans lashed on deck. Special black thermal bags which are left out in the sun filled with water are an easy way of having a supply of hot water without electricity.

A large plastic bowl can act as a baby bath and double up for washing clothes, but this is yet one more bulky item to find storage space for. There are some space saving baths available, such as an inflatable bath, or a plastic sheet bath, where a heavy plastic sheet is suspended on a frame which can be unclipped and folded away. On *Aventura* we installed a large domestic size stainless steel sink in the galley, as all sinks made for boats appeared to us to be extremely small, whether for washing dishes or a child.

Some ingenuity may be needed to control the amount of water used, but a baby does not get very dirty at sea and it is not necessary to bath a baby every day. Face, hands and bottom can be kept clean without using a lot of water and, if fresh water is very limited, a sponge down is a perfectly adequate alternative. The washing water can be used easily for something else such as soaking the nappies.

Transferring young children safely on, off or between boats requires care and attention, preferably with both hands free.

Thinking of dual purposes for items can also help to reduce the amount of gear carried, for it is all too easy to be buried under mounds of baby chairs, cots, baths, pushchairs, toys, etc. It is worth considering very seriously if some of these items can be dispensed with while living on board.

Transporting baby

The most hazardous moments when cruising with a small baby are getting on and off the boat, especially from a dinghy while at anchor. There is little room on most boats for prams or pushchairs, even the folding stroller variety, so methods of carrying the child about the body are popular with boating parents.

The slings and carriers for babies either carry the child in front of the body or on the back. For the tiny baby, the soft sling that holds the baby close to the chest is probably the most convenient. The baby feels content near to the parental heartbeat and it is easier for the parent to see how the child is. These fabric slings are like a pouch; some have a neck support for the newborn and others have a protective outer cover which zips around the carrier seat. An older child who is heavier may be more tiring to carry in front and, if the baby can already keep his back straight in a sitting position and does not need his head supported, a backpack type of carrier may be more suitable. It is certainly easier to carry a heavy infant for longer periods in this way. On the back the baby is more exposed and one cannot keep an eye on what he is doing, but it does give an older baby a better view of the world. Some of these backpacks with rigid frames can also be used as a baby seat, which can justify the extra space they take compared to the foldable fabric slings.

The advantage of all these types of carrier is that they leave both the parents' hands free for getting on or off the boat, carrying shopping or whatever. With baby in front, all one has to be careful of is not to bump the child as one climbs aboard, but as the child is close and visible this is not difficult to avoid. When leaning forward it is safer to cradle the baby's head with one hand.

Some parents feel that the baby is more protected if transported in his basket or carrycot, but this is a two handed operation and not so easy to attempt on one's own. When handing a child up and down in this way from dinghy to boat, it is essential that one has a firm stable footing. The dinghy should be attached both fore and aft securely with short painters and one must be careful not to push the dinghy away from the boat as one hands up the baby and cot. In this operation there will only be one hand free to steady oneself against the side of the boat.

Babies do not have the same capacity for temperature regulation as adults and so are more susceptible to the extremes of the weather. Also they have no way of communicating if they are too hot or too cold apart from crying. Care must be taken to protect small children from too much cold, especially wind or spray when transporting them over water. The sun should be treated with equal caution, for tender young skins and eyes are particularly vulnerable and direct exposure to strong sunlight should be as brief as possible for babies. Some exposure is unavoidable when going to and fro, although a cotton sun hat with a brim to shade the eyes is easily worn. As fresh air is so beneficial one does not want to keep a baby inside the boat all the time, so a canopy or awning should be rigged up over the cockpit when the sun is strong. A large cockpit awning is essential for cruising in sunny climes and even while sailing some protection for a child can be easily rigged up with a smaller piece of canvas.

Frances Stocks of *Kleena Kleene II* particularly recommends the use of a sheepskin for a baby to sleep on. By trapping air, it provides insulation when it is cold and helps the baby's skin to keep cool when the weather is hot. Frances found it invaluable, as her daughter Brandi would sleep anywhere in the boat and under any conditions as long as she was on her sheepskin. A sheepskin does not need to be washed as often as one would imagine.

Amusing a small child

A deterrent to many parents contemplating making a passage or spending a longer time cruising must be the prospect of amusing a small child at sea. Small babies are no problem, as rocked by the wave motion they are probably happier than on shore. Eyecatching mobiles strung up in their line of vision will amuse them as the mobiles move with the movement of the boat.

A small chair into which an infant can be securely strapped is also useful, not only for feeding the baby, but so that he can see what is going on inside the boat instead of lying gazing at the ceiling. Similar to a seat for immobilising a toddler, an infant's chair must be firmly secured or anchored in some way, so that the lurch of a wave does not tip the baby out or the chair over. Some chairs have a small tray which can be fixed in front of the child to hold toys or a plate when a baby starts to feed himself. Due to the increase in travel by all means, not only on the water, there are various portable high chairs or adaptable seats on the market. One simple portable chair clamps onto any solid table, yet folds away quite small when not in use. This type of chair is only suitable for a child who can already sit unaided, and unless the child can be securely strapped in he should not be left in such a chair unattended.

The same toys that amuse a small child ashore will amuse him afloat as well, and although children do differ in their tastes, most acquire one favourite cuddly soft toy which should never be left behind. There is normally plenty of activity and movement on a boat to catch the attention of an infant and until a baby becomes mobile there are few problems in amusing him. Once a child can crawl or walk the difficulties begin and some children find it very restricting to spend a lot of time in the confines of a boat instead of running, jumping and being active as they would be on shore. Children vary enormously in character, some being more active than others, but generally smaller children have less capacity to amuse themselves than older children. They may well demand the attention of an adult to read a story, sing nursery rhymes or play games with them.

The British couple Sylvia and Ian French considered that amusing their son John took most of their spare time, especially on passage, during the three years they spent circumnavigating in their 27 foot sloop *Pomona*. Along with keeping watches and the general work involved in running a boat, amusing John meant that they had little time left to do other things. They had planned their world cruise while John was small so as to be back home in time for him to commence school at five. Later, on reflection, they considered this was not so important as they had originally thought and that sailing with him at an older age might have been more rewarding.

Similarly, the task of occupying their two daughters under five was one of the main reasons why Vicki and John Holmes of *Korong II* returned home to Australia to live ashore after a two year cruise in the Pacific. Several years earlier,

Playing with young Kevin takes a lot of Françoise Pitteloud's time, especially at sea.

before they had children, they had undertaken another extensive cruise and so noticed the difference that children made. Attentiveness to the young girls' safety and keeping them amused left little time for the parents to enjoy themselves how they would have liked to. Although 43 foot *Korong II* was a spacious well-equipped boat, fitted out with young children in mind and even with a washing machine on board, Vicki Holmes still found life afloat with a couple of under-fives very exhausting. The Holmes' grumble that they could rarely go out of an evening was echoed by Max Fletcher of *Christopher Robin*, who also complained that babysitters were not easy to come by when living afloat.

Although there are special problems in sailing with the very young, a little thought and organisation can easily surmount them, much depending on the attitude of mind of the parents. In the survey of long distance voyagers we carried out in the Pacific, out of the twenty children on fourteen boats, ten were under the age of five and four of these had been born since the start of their parents' voyage. These children had all grown up knowing little else except the sailing life and were well adapted to life on a boat. As they knew nothing else, they regarded life on a boat as normal and nothing special at all. Perhaps cruising with infants was best summed up by Max Fletcher of *Christopher Robin*, whose son Christopher was only nine months old when the Fletchers set sail from Maine

73

on the east coast of the United States in their Westsail 32. When I spoke to him in New Zealand, Max told me, 'Cruising with a young child was so much easier than I thought it was going to be.'

7
Making the Most of a Holiday Cruise

As an increasing number of parents take their children to sea, there comes a point when something a little more exciting than a day trip beckons across the horizon. Even the most dedicated racing enthusiast may decide to change his style for a family holiday. While some families may be content to potter around the shores of their home area, others may prefer to take a cruise that is a little more adventurous, and there are few children who do not enjoy the excitement of going to foreign places. From the south and east coast of England, France, Holland or Belgium are but a day's sail away, while Mexico beckons to the Californian and down-east from New England leads to Canada.

Another possibility for making a change from the home cruising area is to take a charter holiday, which also may be one way to decide if the family really likes cruising before investing in a suitable boat. The number and diversity of bareboat charter companies has risen dramatically in recent years, offering the attractions of cruising in beautiful faraway places without the expense and time involved in taking one's own boat there. Flotilla sailing among the Greek islands and bareboat chartering in the Caribbean are the two most popular cruising holidays, although charter operations are to be found almost anywhere the cruising is good, from Tahiti to Tonga, Yugoslavia to the Great Barrier Reef in Australia.

The more exotic is, of course, the more expensive and some parents may have doubts about whether it is worthwhile to spend such money on a family holiday.

Nevertheless sailing in an area where the weather is sunnier and more predictable is a great attraction for those living in colder climes. Children may learn to enjoy sailing much more readily when the air is warm, the sea temperature perfect for swimming and when any spray that comes on board is warm spray. Whatever kind of cruising one does, whether one splashes out on a charter holiday or is content to enjoy the known pleasures of home waters, it is still worth making some effort to ensure that a child both enjoys himself and gains from the experience.

Jobs for children

The first step in fostering a child's interest in sailing is to involve him as much as possible in the sailing of the boat. This not only keeps the child busy and occupied, but also gives a sense of achievement and pride in mastering the skills involved. One way of increasing a child's sense of participation is to designate a particular job as that child's sole responsibility.

Even quite young children can be found jobs to do, such as scrubbing the decks or tidying and coiling ropes. When they were small, my children enjoyed making a round cheese of the sheets on the aft deck, particularly winding the large main sheet very carefully. With all the ropes neatly coiled or decoratively wound, it meant our boat looked shipshape too. Putting on the sail covers and lacing them up when one arrives in port is another job that fairly young children can manage to do successfully, and two small ones can help each other if the cover is too bulky for one to manage alone. Learning to tie proper knots is something that most children enjoy, from putting a simple figure of eight in the end of a sheet to the more complicated bowline on a mooring line. Once one is satisfied with their knot tying skills, children can get on with tasks such as tying on fenders, while even those not trusted with knots can easily take the fenders off and pack them away tidily.

Early in our cruising life, my son Ivan was designated the flag officer, with the responsibility of raising and lowering our ensign, courtesy and code flags, and folding them away neatly. He took this job very seriously, especially after we acquired a complete set of code flags, learning all the letters, codes and how to dress the ship overall in the correct fashion. Identifying the flags of other countries became one of his hobbies, although the skipper of a small motor boat in Sicily, flying the Panamanian flag of convenience to avoid local taxes, did not appreciate being told by a six year old that he was flying it upside down. Ivan kept a flag folder as part of his school work, drawing and colouring each new flag he spotted, making a note of where and on what vessel he had seen it. He also found out about the origins of some of the flags which often reflect the history of the country concerned.

76

An older child of seven or eight can handle the jib sheet if the wind is not too strong or alternatively can tail for an adult pulling in the sheet. Selftailing winches are an aid as far as children are concerned because they can be operated with two hands. Sometimes my two children would pull together on the sheet so as to gain the necessary muscle power. Handling the jib sheet when the sail is hoisted, or adjusting it when the point of sailing is changed, is one job that a child can do without going on deck but from safely inside the cockpit and still feel a sense of participation in the sailing of the boat.

A small sail such as the mizzen or a staysail can be given over entirely to a child as his responsibility. If the sail area is not too large or if it is a sail used only in lighter airs, the child can feel the satisfaction of hauling it up and setting it correctly, maybe even learning to decide when it should go up or come down, depending on the point of sailing or weather conditions. After a few years of sailing, I made a mizzen staysail to help push our heavily laden boat along a little faster in lighter breezes. Doina and Ivan took this sail over completely as their sail and were in charge of hoisting it, although as it was a three handed operation they did employ the skipper on one of the sheets. To set a large sail correctly needs more strength than most children are likely to possess, but if they are enthusiastic to try, let them hoist as much as they can before an adult tightens those last few inches.

From around ten or twelve years old, children can be a positive help on a boat, no longer mere passengers but able to share in the work load. That means that if one parent is off watch and snoozing in the daytime, he or she need not be wakened if a sail needs changing, a bonus on a longer passage. By the time children are teenagers they should be capable of being full members of the crew, tackling nearly all the tasks of handling sails and boatwork that an adult would.

Nearly all children love to take the helm and even the youngest can have a closely supervised turn, although he may need some extra lift in the way of cushions so that he can see where he is going. If there are points of interest, such as buoys to round or a shoreline to follow, the child's attention can often be held for longer periods before he gets tired or bored. There is a lot of satisfaction to be had by children at the wheel or tiller, for it does make them feel that they are in charge and that the boat is under their control.

On many cruising boats the helm will be taken over by the automatic pilot or selfsteering gear, but an equal feeling of being in charge can be obtained by the child standing a watch. Among the many families I have met cruising, almost all the children over the age of ten or eleven took full daytime watches. Sometimes two younger children stood a watch together, while older teenagers also stood a night watch, often the first one of the evening. Children usually respond very well to being given responsibility and take the jobs they are given very seriously. Start by giving a child a short watch of maybe half an hour and keep an unobtrusive eye on how attentive the child is being, checking that he is not too easily distracted into playing games or reading. It is helpful if the circumstances when the watchkeeper should alert the skipper are explained carefully, such as another vessel approaching, sighting land or a buoy, or the appearance of a threatening black cloud.

Navigation is another subject in which it is easy to arouse the interest of children and which they usually enjoy because it enables them to follow the progress of a cruise more closely. Even those children who do not enjoy sailing all that much can be quite keen to find out how soon the destination will be reached. Most children are fascinated by charts and pore over them, picking out landmarks they have recognised, or puzzle over identifying a certain rock, island or other feature. Checking the number on a buoy with binoculars or timing a light with a stopwatch can be fun, not a chore. Quite early on, my children learnt how to use the handbearing compass and with a little help could transfer their readings into lines on the chart to pinpoint our position. Ivan became so interested that he mastered using the sextant, too, and by the age of ten could take a reasonably accurate noon sight and work out our position. A cheaper plastic sextant that we had as a back up was given over to him, so he could take sights in parallel with his father and compare results.

Some of the tasks the children undertook were not strictly necessary but just an interesting diversion. A favourite was to estimate the speed of the boat by one child dropping a piece of paper off the bow and the other child timing its arrival at the stern with the stopwatch. From the time taken for the paper to travel the length of the boat, the speed can be calculated. If the paper takes x seconds to travel the length of the boat (y), it would travel $60/x \times y$ feet in 1 minute. Multiplying this figure by 60 gives the distance travelled in 1 hour. For example, if the paper took 5 seconds to travel the length of a 35 foot boat, it would travel $60/x \times 35 \times 60$ feet in 1 hour. To find the speed in knots, the distance travelled is divided by the number of feet in a nautical mile (6,080) For the example quoted above this works at 4.14 knots.

The rapid development of electronic equipment in recent years has brought about a large change in what a boat will be equipped with, particularly as regards navigation. Many parents may well find that their children, brought up in a technological age, turn out to be more at home with onboard computers or GPS systems than they are themselves. Older children may also come to use the radio like a telephone. During the ARC transatlantic rally in 1990, in which some 120 yachts crossed the Atlantic from the Canary Islands to the Caribbean, 17 year old Samantha Hill sailing on *Kirtonia* with her family, including a younger brother and sister, ran a children's radio net, keeping in touch over the airwaves with other boats with children on board.

If instruments such as depth sounders are down below at the navigation station, children can be useful messengers in relaying data such as the depth to the skipper on deck, who maybe is carefully looking out for dangers when coming in to anchor, or so he knows how much anchor chain to let out. Our standard method of coming into an unknown lagoon in areas of coral reef or coral heads was for Jimmy to climb the mast while I remained at the wheel, unfortunately out of hearing because of our wheelhouse. This was solved by stationing one of the children on the aft deck to relay the skipper's commands, 'ten degrees to port', 'ten degrees to starboard', or 'keep straight ahead'.

It is not only the fun side of sailing that children can take part in: they should also help with the less popular tasks too. That inevitably means the washing of the dishes, which appears to be the least popular chore on a boat as well as on shore. Our two children took it in turns to wash up, one taking odd dates and the other evens, with Jimmy solving the problem of 31 day months by doing that day himself. Many children enjoy cooking, but this is one job that has to be handled very carefully when at sea because of the danger of scalding. Yet even that can be solved in some way or another, such as an enthusiastic young cook making a cake, which the adult supervises putting in and taking out of the oven. For younger children it might be wiser to restrict their culinary activities to when one is in port or at anchor.

Involving the children fully in all aspects of life on board is an excellent way of counteracting any boredom that might result from being confined in a restricted space at sea. The lack of space is most noticeable where active children are concerned and never so much of a problem with the kind of child who is happy curled up in a corner with a good book, whether he is at home or at sea. Children vary enormously in temperament and character, so that there can be no hard rules; an activity which is perfect for one child can be a pain for another. Certainly if one's child is happy reading on his bunk or listening to his favourite music tapes, there is no merit in forcing him into spending a lot of time on deck.

While at sea the opportunities for an active child are more limited; in port or at anchor there are plenty of activities where a child can expend excess energy, from swimming to rowing the dinghy. The challenge of climbing the mast is regarded as a great sport by many sailing children and we have motored into several anchorages in calm weather with two children perched on our spreaders. Like little monkeys, children swing from ropes and sheets or play in the rigging and ratlines, especially on larger, older boats with heavier gear. Even on a smaller boat, the bosun's chair shackled onto the mainsail halyard can make a swing that will keep a child occupied for quite a while.

Another marvellous pastime is that of spinnaker flying, but warm water is essential for this or else a hardy constitution. The anchoring arrangement of the boat has to be changed so that it is anchored or moored from the stern, with the stern into the wind. A bosun's chair or similar canvas seat is then suspended between the two tacks of the spinnaker or cruising chute. Climbing into the seat in the water and stretching apart the tacks with the hands, the person is lifted up to fly above the water as the wind fills the sail. How high one flies depends on

Doina spinnaker flying in Tonga, a sport that most cruising children enjoy.

the strength of the wind and one's weight, although the spinnaker halyard can be payed out to increase this height a little. In fact, a light breeze which will not lift a grown man out of the water is ideal for children, whereas the stronger winds needed to give a man a good ride can lift a child frighteningly high. A line attached to one tack and left slack can be used to bring down a child who has had enough – or more likely one who refuses to give anyone else a chance.

Diaries and logbooks

After participating in sailing the boat, one of the most rewarding things a child can do is to keep a diary or logbook of his cruise. A special book can be bought and its cover decorated with illustrations, photographs or designs, with the title of the cruise in bold letters. Books with both lined and unlined pages are ideal so there is space for both drawings and descriptions. Alternatively a file can be used so that the number of pages can be easily added to and different kinds of paper utilised. A smaller child might use a book that has half a page plain for drawing with a few lines underneath on which he can write about his drawing. As well as drawings, the diary can be illustrated with postcards of places visited ashore, or entrance tickets to museums, even bus tickets. An older child who takes his own photographs could use these to illustrate his diary. For the little ones not yet able to write, the same idea can be followed in a scrapbook with big coloured plain pages. They can be helped to paste in postcards, tickets and any other bits and pieces they may have collected ashore. Cutting out the pictures from tourist brochures is another colourful source for illustrating a scrapbook.

There are many variations in what can go into such a book, depending on a child's age and interests, from drawing and identifying marine life to the history of places visited. Sometimes my children's diaries were more of a catalogue of what they ate or the games they had devised for their own amusement than the sights they had seen, but those were things that were important for them. A particular harbour might be remembered for the fact that it had a shop on the quay selling delicious icecream rather than for the castle guarding the entrance.

Some older children may prefer to keep their logbooks more in the style of a ship's log, in which they can note the distance travelled, wind speed and weather conditions, lighthouses or buoys passed, or the names of other vessels seen at sea. If the cruise area is rich in history, as many of the European coastlines or the New England coastline of America are, the diary or scrapbook can help to keep the historical sites visited fresh in the children's memory. Cruising guides which give some of this history or other books about the places visited are useful to have on board to stimulate an interest in the area being cruised in.

Not only does a child get more out of cruising by keeping such a diary, but it also remains as a treasured momento, something to show to friends when one returns home. My children have kept diaries in various places and always got great enjoyment and much hilarity out of rereading them at a later date.

Hobbies and interests

Cruising also offers an ideal opportunity for extending a child's special interest or hobby, as well as introducing new pastimes which a child may not have thought of before or had the opportunity to pursue. Starry nights in the cockpit with the pair of binoculars that almost all boats possess could well stimulate an interest in astronomy or at least in identifying stars, planets and constellations. A good map of the night sky or a star finder is essential and the easiest way to learn the constellations is to identify one or two of the well known groups, such as Orion or the Great Bear, and then work out other constellations from their position in relation to these. Few navigators nowadays use the stars, and with the advent of satellite navigation probably even less will in the future, but the subject may still catch the imagination of a child intrigued by how the sailors of yesteryear found their way across the oceans without the instruments of today.

As mentioned earlier, spotting flags of different countries or code flags is another hobby that some children might like to follow. We also had a little book, *I-Spy at Sea*, which gave points for different kinds of ships, buoys, lighthouses and other features that could be spied at sea. If there is more than one child on board, these spotting games can be run as a friendly competition. Another idea for this kind of observation game is to collect unusual boat names.

Children are often avid collectors and those who already collect stamps, matchbox labels or who press wild flowers will find plenty of opportunities to collect other items too. Beachcombing among the flotsam and jetsam yields all kinds of unlikely items, from glass fishing floats to wood or glass eroded into peculiar shapes by the action of wave and water, as well as a wide variety of natural objects from seaweed and egg cases to shells and pretty pebbles.

Shell collecting

One of the most popular hobbies among sailing children is collecting shells, whether scavenged from beaches or collected by swimming underwater. To increase a child's interest it is worth buying a book on shells, so the child can try to identify the specimens he collects or at least classify them into their families. Background information on various shells will also help to make the collection more interesting. The true collector will keep a record not only of the name of the shell, but where it was found, the type of habitat and depth of water.

Make sure that shell-gathering is permitted in your cruising area. In the Seychelles it is illegal to collect any shells from specified shell reserves.

The shells found on the seashore and even many of those in the sea will be dead and empty, but some collected by diving or in rockpools will still have the owner inside. Cleaning these living shells can be quite a problem. The simplest method is to gently heat the shells in fresh water, then prise the dead animal out with a pin, bent wire or other suitable utensil, such as one uses for eating shellfish or snails. Unfortunately this method cannot be used on the porcelain type shells such as cowries or olives, because heating them makes the shiny glaze go cloudy or crack and so ruins their beauty. For these shells there is no simple solution. I usually waited for them to die by leaving them out of water, then tried to remove as much as possible of the dead animal with a jet of water and various implements. Then I suspended them from the side of the boat in a mesh string bag. Gradually fish and other small creatures devoured the remains. The whole operation can be quite odiferous and a poor sense of smell is a great advantage.

This problem of cleaning shells was one of the reasons why we did not take too many of a particular species, although the more attractive shells did make appreciated presents for friends. The main reason, though, is so as not to denude an area, but to leave plenty of shells to create the following generations. For a similar reason any stones or slabs that have been turned over to look for shells should be turned back again, because minute eggs and other small creatures may be on the underside and will perish if exposed. Shell collecting has become so popular that unfortunately whole areas have been virtually stripped clean by commercially minded people who have only their own profit in view and not any conservation of the species. Therefore it is very important to teach children not to take more than they need. This is sometimes difficult when a pretty variety is in apparent abundance. In a lagoon in the Society Islands, Doina and Ivan discovered they could track down the long pointed auger shells by following their trail through the sand to where they had buried themselves. The children became so fascinated by the success of their detective work and their free diving prowess, that in the end I had to call a halt to their collection of this species.

The only shells that can be harmful are a few species of the cone family, which release a small dart to kill their prey. This dart contains a poisonous substance which has been known to be fatal, particularly from the white and brown blotched *conus geographicus*. It is prudent to take hold of all cone shells from the back, keeping the aperture pointing away, and then any dart is released away from the body. The majority of cone shells are harmless and the cone family is one of the most popular among collectors, as it has such a striking variety of colours, pattern and shapes. It is also prudent never to walk barefoot on a reef and to look very carefully before touching anything or turning over stones, keeping fingers out of open clam shells. A small stick can easily be used instead for turning over stones or prodding into gloomy corners.

Monitoring marine mammals

There can be few cruising children who do not welcome the company of dolphins and enjoy watching these beautiful animals riding the bow wave or disporting themselves beside the boat. Some children may be interested in taking this diversion a little more seriously by acting as observers for organisations which are interested in sightings of dolphins and whales. These organisations, usually university research groups, provide forms on which to record the information they require, and they also have available guides to the identification of cetaceans, which is the family name for dolphins and whales. There are a surprisingly large number of species, the common dolphin being only one of some 25 species which have been sighted in the North Atlantic area alone.

The most important features to record are the estimated size of the animals, the shape of the head and snout, the size, shape and position of the dorsal fin and, in the case of whales, the size and shape of blow. Identifying the exact species is not easy, especially in rougher weather, and even experienced observers can have difficulty, so it is far better to record simply 'dolphin species' along with the description of as many features as can be seen, including body colour and markings. Other information which is important is the exact location of the sighting (latitude and longitude), the date and GMT time, the number of animals in a group and the presence of any young animals, their direction of travel and behaviour, such as jumping or bowriding, as well as any seabirds associated with them. Details of weather conditions, such as wind direction, force, state of the sea, wave height and visibility, are also important. Even reporting areas of the ocean where no dolphins or whales were seen is of value to scientists evaluating all the data they receive.

Concern over endangered species, such as whales or sea-turtles has grown over the last few years, spearheaded by organisations such as Greenpeace or Friends of the Earth. Interested children may well enjoy taking part in some of the programmes which involve logging marine mammals observed. Whaleforce is one such programme, which is aimed specifically at the pleasure boater and sailor.

Further information can be obtained from:

UK Cetacean Group, Edward Grey Institute, South Parks Road, Oxford, OX1 3PS, England.

International Dolphin Watch, Department of Anatomy, Downing Street, Cambridge, CB2 3DY England.

Division of Mammals, Smithsonian Institution, National Museum of Natural History, Washington, DC 20560, USA.

College of the Atlantic, Bar Harbor, Maine, USA.

Dolphin Survey Project

Report Form

Send to : Mr D.A. McBrearty, M.A.,
Dolphin Survey Project,
Dept. of Anatomy,
University of Cambridge,
Downing Street,
Cambridge, CB2 3DY.

Name of Observer: ....

Vessel: ....

Address: ....
....

Behaviour/Activity pattern of dolphin: feeding, playing, bowriding, leaping; shape of school pattern. How close are the animals and do they show any interest in your vessel?

INTERNATIONAL DOLPHIN WATCH

Date: .... Time: .... GMT .... Local.

Ships position Lat .... Long ....

Weather Conditions: .... Sea Temp ....

Number seen: Adults .... Juveniles ....

Estimate of length .... Juveniles ....

Species ....

Observed characteristics from which identification is made. eg. colour pattern, shape of dorsal fin, flipper shape, type of beak (long, short or absent).

Please try to make a sketch of the animal you see.

is a photograph/slide/film available ....

Hubbs Sea World Research Institute, 1700 South Shore Road, San Diego, CA 92109, USA

National Fisheries Service, Southwest Fisheries Center, La Jolla, CA 92058 USA.

Whaleforce, Erth Barton, Elm Gate, Saltash, Cornwall PL12 4QY, England and PO Box 484, Cochrane, Alberta, Canada TOL OWO.

Archie Carr Center for Sea Turtle Research, University of Florida, Gainesville, FL 32611, USA.

Center for Marine Conservation, 1725 DeSales Street, NW, Washington DC 20036, USA.

Apart from shell collecting or dolphin spotting, many children may like to take a more serious interest in any marine life encountered, whether it is identifying a fish caught at the end of the line or seabirds skimming over the waves. Useful additions to the shipboard bookshelf are small reference books on seabirds, fish and other marine life, both that found along the seashore as well as on the high seas. It is amazing how much there is to observe if one does keep one's eyes open – not only seabirds or fish, but brightly coloured sea snakes wriggling along, turtles lazily basking on the surface or the gauzy blue butterfly wings of the by-the-wind-sailor. The keen young naturalist might like to keep a notebook with detailed descriptions and drawings of the wildlife he observes, much in the style of the dolphin sightings.

Marine conservation

As well as taking an interest in helping to preserve endangered species or logging whales and dolphins, many children may be interested in other aspects of preserving the marine environment. A major coordinator of such projects in the USA is the Washington-based Center for Marine Conservation (address above). The Center publishes an ocean activity book for children, *The Ocean: Consider the Connnections*, which contains a wide variety of marine education activities for all ages. As well as ocean wildlife projects, there are several ongoing projects concerning monitoring debris floating in the oceans, the disposal of onboard rubbish, particularly plastics, and children have also been involved in various coastal cleanups. Many children take a lively interest in environmental matters, and as the pollution of our oceans is something that will affect their future sailing, this interest should be actively encouraged.

Fishing

Fishing is an ideal occupation to pursue while afloat, whether the child hangs hook and line over the side while at anchor or trawls behind the boat while sailing. The latter method can result in some quite large catches when the assistance of an adult may well be required. Small children need careful supervision when using fish hooks because when these become embedded in fingers or hands they can necessitate a hospital visit for their removal. An alternative for the younger enthusiast is to attach a net to a long stick, which can also be used in shallow waters along a beach or for retrieving lost objects. Underwater fishing with a spear gun is better left to older teenagers who can be trusted to operate this equipment safely.

All the forms of fishing, from rod and line to nets or spearguns, do provide great satisfaction for children, especially when the catch is suitable and large enough to be eaten. Similarly providing the family dinner by collecting mussels, cockles or other shellfish can be an occasion of pride.

Sports

Many older teenage children who sail become proficient fishermen both above and under the water. Snorkelling and diving are also popular pastimes among these children. Diving with air tanks does require proper training and should never be attempted by an untrained person. If a young person does become interested in sub-aqua diving, there are many clubs and organisations where professional training can be received. However, even a beginner who is just

A tender which can be rigged for sailing gives children a lot of pleasure.

learning to swim can don mask, snorkel and flippers and so discover the beauty of underwater scenery, even if only looking down from the surface. All of this equipment can now be bought in small sizes, and snorkelling might provide just the incentive needed for a youngster to improve his capability in the water. Many of the children I have met who have been cruising in warmer waters for any length of time have been very able free divers, spending as much time exploring under the water as swimming on the surface.

All the water related sports are easily pursued from a boat and many charter companies provide not only scuba gear of flippers, masks and snorkels for their clients but also equip their boats with sailboards. Recently the sport of sailboarding has greatly expanded and many boats now find space on their decks to store a sailboard. Many of the latest boards are not easily handled by a younger person and a certain strength is required of a child before he can pull the sail and wishbone up out of the water, although there are some junior boards on the market. A small sailing dinghy might be more easily managed by the younger members of the crew and has the advantage that more than one child can enjoy themselves in it at the same time, instead of waiting for turns. Finding space to stow a sailing dinghy is one of the biggest problems on all but the largest boats, although some of the smaller sized dinghies such as the Optimist will fit on the foredeck or coachroof and can double as a tender. Some inflatable dinghies can also be rigged to sail and this might be an attractive alternative for family cruising.

Children do get great pleasure out of messing about in the dinghy, whether they sail or row, especially when this gives them the chance to do some exploring on their own of inlets and other corners of a harbour. Obviously one should be satisfied that the children are capable rowers or can handle the sails before letting them venture too far afield. While a dinghy that can be rigged for sailing or one that rows well is a boon while cruising with children, it then becomes almost essential to have a second dinghy, even if only the smallest inflatable. Otherwise one is likely to find oneself marooned on a boat at anchor when the children have disappeared both out of sight and out of hearing, which I know from experience can be extremely frustrating.

In this chapter I have tried to outline some of the ways that children can enjoy themselves while on a cruise, helping to sail the boat, keeping a logbook or diary and pursuing various hobbies or sports. By making the most of their holiday or short cruise they will be well on the way to becoming enthusiastic sailors with enduring memories of their experiences.

8
On Passage

Making a longer passage has to be considered as soon as one thinks about cruising further afield. Even if not absolutely necessary, it is often the quickest way to get to one's destination instead of hopping along the coast and stopping every night. Especially if time is limited, many families might consider a longer passage at the beginning or end of their holiday to allow more days in their chosen cruising area. The idea of a longer passage may well cause cruising parents to hesitate as they wonder how they are going to amuse their offspring out of sight of land. The two problems that immediately come to mind are boredom and the confinement of an active child to the restricted space of a boat. Children who are normally very energetic and do a lot of swimming, other sports or just running about, may find being cooped up on a small boat for several days or even longer rather frustrating. Providing an outlet for their energy is not easy, and there is no quick solution to this problem. The key lies in keeping them fully occupied and involved in other things, so that the other problem of boredom has less time to rear its head.

If the weather is fairly benign children can be quite active, not only inside the boat but also out in the cockpit or on deck, harnessed if necessary. When the weather deteriorates even the most lively child usually slows down and many children are content to spend more time in their bunks, especially if they have any feelings of seasickness. Involving the children in as much of the sailing of the boat as possible not only gives an outlet for their energies but also gives them the feeling of being needed and useful. Many of the ways in which children can help on a boat were outlined in the previous chapter, from washing up and cooking

The locks of the Panama Canal provide an interesting diversion after a long passage.

to handling smaller sails, jib sheets and giving a helping hand, such as by finding a shackle key, passing a winch handle or sail ties. Children over the age of ten usually take at least a short daytime watch on most boats, which is a considerable help for a shorthanded crew. The length of time a child spends on watch, or if an evening or night watch is also stood, depends on the maturity and age of the child. Generally it is only children from about fourteen upwards who stand watches in the hours of darkness.

For children who are on a more lengthy cruise there will be schoolwork to be done, which occupies some of the day, the number of hours depending on the age of the child. On many cruising boats the children prefer to do more schoolwork on passage, not only to counteract boredom but to earn themselves time off when they reach port. On the other hand a few children do very little schoolwork at sea – mainly those who suffer from seasickness to some degree. A certain amount of flexibility has to be shown on passage, taking into account the particular child, even if the correspondence course followed requires work to be returned by a set date. Several of the parents who teach their children themselves vary the school routine at sea and include more oral work and reading, and less written tasks. In this way Doina and Ivan learnt their multiplication tables on passage as well as such items as French verbs and spellings. We kept longer writing projects for in port and never attempted chemistry experiments or anything of that nature at sea.

Special projects

There are many special projects that can be carried out on a passage, whether as part of the school routine or as a way of adding interest to the passage for children who do not have to do schoolwork. A typical project is to take daily weather recordings, which is something my children did on our Atlantic crossing. At the same time each day, the wind speed and direction can be measured, either by reading the electronic instruments on board, or by a small handheld wind speed indicator, which also incorporates a compass. The air and sea temperatures can also be measured; for the latter, the adult should fetch up a bucket of seawater into the cockpit, so the child can take the water temperature in safety. The temperature of the sea is especially interesting if one is sailing into an area of changing temperature, as when crossing the Gulf Stream. Other points which can be noted are the type of clouds and the appearance of the sky, the estimated height of waves and their appearance and the presence or absence of foam on their tops. If there are not suitable instruments on board, a child might like to devise his own method of measurement, such as making a rudimentary wind vane attached to a compass, or a simple rainfall gauge.

The results can be plotted in various forms, from a simple line graph with a cross showing the particular value recorded for each day to more complicated variations. Block graphs appeal more to children as the different items can be blocked in with different colours. A child can amuse himself in deciding how to make his weather chart, maybe giving different colours to different winds or, as Doina did, using little arrows to show wind direction. At the end of the passage an older child could construct a pie chart (a circle with segments corresponding to proportions) to show the percentage of winds encountered from different quarters. This type of weather recording appeals more to an older child, although a younger child can easily make a simple weather chart by drawing and colouring a symbol for each day – a yellow sun, clouds, rain or lots of wind – or alternatively cutting out symbols from coloured paper. However complicated or simple the chart is, it still serves as a permanent record of the passage for the child to keep. Watching the temperature rise or the number of yellow suns on the chart increase as one sails towards warmer places gives an incentive to everyone in the crew, not only the children.

Older children might also like to learn to navigate, to use a sextant and work out the boat's position. A second plastic sextant is a useful acquisition, both as a backup and for a child to learn with. Even if the navigator now uses satellite navigation methods, a child can still plot his own course alongside, challenged to see how accurate he can get. Using his navigation results and reading distances covered off the log, the child could mark in a track of the passage on a chart or a copy of a chart, even drawing in little symbols for events that occurred, such as strong winds, a thunderstorm or dolphins bowriding.

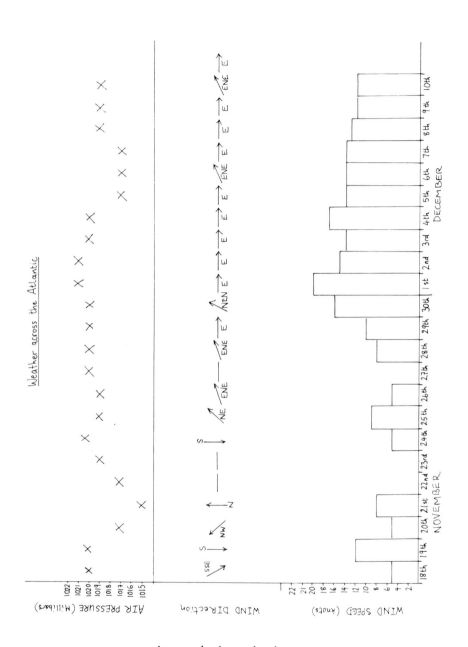

An example of a weather chart.

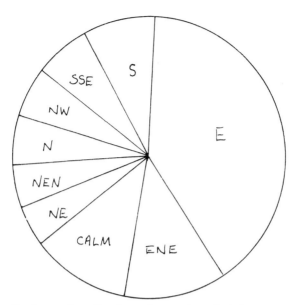

Pie chart to show direction and proportions of winds on a passage.

The young ones

Many of these projects are obviously more suitable for older children and not applicable to those not yet able to read or write. Such small children will also not be capable of taking part in any of the boatwork and watchkeeping and the onus of entertaining them lies heavily with the adults. Having more than one child does ease the problem, especially if they are close enough in age to play together. Sometimes it is not even playing, as Nina and Juan Ribas of *Abuelo III* explained when I asked how three year old Luisa occupied her time on passage. 'Mainly bothering her one year old brother,' was the reply.

Some aspects of amusing the very young were discussed in the chapter on babies and infants and a certain amount of time will have to be spent by parents reading stories and playing games with the children. This can be tiring when sailing shorthanded, but fortunately younger children do also usually sleep longer on passage. Space should be found for as many toys and games as possible, and particularly for the child's favourite soft toys. If a child is surrounded by his familiar toys from at home, not only does he feel more secure but there is no reason why he should not play and occupy himself as he would ashore.

Reading

Once a child has learnt to read and can enjoy a good book, life for the parents often becomes much easier. When I asked parents taking part in the ocean cruising surveys how their children amused themselves on passage, the most frequent answer given was reading. Only one teenager read very little, but occupied herself playing video games, a sign of the changing times. A few years after this survey video machines became commonplace on boats with children on board. The consumption of a book a day was not uncommon, being specifically mentioned by several parents. My daughter Doina was in this category and reaped the benefit of six years without television, as by the end of our cruise, at fourteen years old, she had become an extremely well-read young lady. The biggest problem with these avid readers is keeping up a suitable supply of reading material without lowering the waterline too drastically. This was usually solved by cruising children themselves and 'Have you got any books to trade?' was a familiar opening gambit for making friends on arriving in a new port. As children grow up they can also begin to dip into the adult bookshelf.

Books about the passage, or about other sailors who have sailed the same way in the past, can sometimes tempt a child who does not normally read much. These are interesting books to have on board even for readers who need little tempting, as are books about the place one is sailing to. Popular books with sailing children are those that involve the sea, such as *Two Years Before the Mast* by R.H. Dana or *Round the Horn Before the Mast* by Basil Lubbock, both contemporary accounts of life aboard sailing ships in the last century. *The Kon Tiki Expedition* by Thor Heyerdahl, Joshua Slocum's *Sailing Alone Around the World* and the various accounts of unusual voyages by Captain Villiers are all sea classics which, although not written specifically for children, are not too difficult for a young reader. Some voyages have been retold for younger readers, such as the excellent retelling of Darwin's voyage and work, published by Oxford University Press. In the fiction field, mention must be made of those perennial favourites among sailing children, the *Swallows and Amazons* series by Arthur Ransome, all thick enough to keep a child quiet and absorbed for a reasonable length of time.

Other activities on passage mentioned by cruising parents in the survey were looking at picture books by young non-readers, drawing, colouring and building things with construction toys such as Lego or Meccano. Making models was another pastime that absorbed some children and there is a vast range of kits on the market, from the very simple to the large and complex, so that something suitable can be found for almost any age of child.

Paper and pencil

A large supply of paper, drawing and colouring books, pencils, crayons and felt pens will never go amiss on a passage, and fortunately these items weigh little and do not take up much space. The possibilities with pencil and paper are almost infinite, from the simple pleasure of drawing from one's own imagination to the traditional noughts and crosses or various word games. There are books for children containing puzzles of all kinds from joining dots to crosswords and anagrams. Older children might like the challenge of making up their own crosswords – not as easy as it appears.

A pad of Altair designs will also occupy a child for a considerable time as he picks out the patterns from these complicated printed designs in different colours. Pattern making toys such as Spirograph can also fill time and, like all of the above pursuits, have the advantage that they do not need another person to play with. Similarly, paper folding in the Japanese style of *origami* fascinates many children and will keep those who are interested busy for great lengths of time. Paints can be a messy item on a boat and, except for boxes of block water colours, are best avoided. With the range of felt tipped pens, coloured pencils and other suitable painting sticks available, there is plenty of choice for artistic expression without making too much mess.

There are many games where little else is required except for pencil and paper, such as seeing how many smaller words can be made from one long word chosen at random. For example, 'navigation' can produce van, tan, tang, vang, vain, gain, ingot, nation, tango, etc. Younger children can be given the advantage of being able to use two letter words such as at, it, on and an, while an adult can be penalised by being restricted to only four letter words and upwards. The winner is the person who scores the greatest number of words.

Pinpointing a letter and then writing down a number of predetermined categories beginning with that letter is another universal word game. Categories could include boys' names, girls' names, towns, countries, animals, vegetables, birds and so on.

Another perennial pencil and paper game is that of joining the dots to make squares. A square of dots is drawn and then each player takes it in turn to join two dots together by a line. When a line completes a square the player may put his initial in it and then has the bonus of another go, which towards the end of the game can result in a whole chain of squares being completed by one player. The art of the game is not to draw a line which gives squares to your opponent, and the winner is the player with the most squares completed.

Games that need no equipment

If the motion of the boat is too much for drawing, painting or word games on paper, there are a lot of games that can be played orally, although these do require more than one participant. Many of the kind of games that people play on long journeys by road or train are equally useful on a boat and can be played sitting in the cockpit, or involving the participation of the person at the helm or

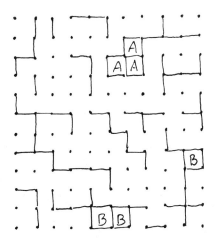

on watch, a useful ploy when the other parent is asleep below. The old favourite I-spy is a little difficult when there is not much else but ocean all around to spy, but there are alternatives. Even the I-spy game can be adapted into a competition to be the first to sight land, a lighthouse or buoy when nearing the end of a voyage.

Baiting a person by firing questions at him which he may not answer with either the words 'yes' or 'no' is popular with all ages, as an unwary adult can be trapped into 'yes' or 'no' without thinking, just as quickly as a child.

Another suggestion is alphabet games, where the players have to think of a town, animal or whatever one chooses for each letter of the alphabet in turn, a player dropping out when he fails to name something. Alternatively each player has to think of something starting with the last letter of the previously mentioned item; again different categories can be used, whether place names, girls' names, flowers or rivers. This can also be played with syllables instead of letters, for example – sailing – ingot – otter – terminal – and so on until a player cannot think of a word. Words already used may not be repeated.

Another simple word game is for each player to add a letter to the previous player's letter, but never to finish a word:

b

bu

bul   (but, bun, bug, would make the player lose)

bulw (bulb, bull, bulk would be losers)

The player must always have a word in mind, which he must give if challenged – in this case, 'bulwark'.

Another word game much enjoyed by most children is memorising a list to which each player adds another item when it is his turn to recite the list. This usually goes something like: 'When my Aunt Dolly went to Peru she took with her a hot water bottle, a pair of purple pyjamas, a mosquito net, a striped umbrella ...' etc.

Board games

Board games such as Scrabble, chess or draughts (checkers), can also pass the time if one has a suitable opponent. Many of these games can be bought in a magnetised variety meant for travelling, very useful at sea where pieces can slide about all too easily. Trivial Pursuit is another currently popular game with many different general knowledge questions to answer. In fact, the cards of this game which have the questions on could be used on their own as a quiz without the board if there was no steady place to play it. My children also enjoyed backgammon, which has the advantage of being played at a faster rate than games like chess and so does not take so long to complete.

There is nothing to beat a pack of playing cards, for taking up the minimum of storage space and providing an almost endless variety of games. I am not going to give details of the many card games or patiences that can be played, as there are many books which do this so much better. Books on card games, word games and pencil and paper games might be worth adding to the boat bookshelf to provide ideas when inspiration fails.

Devising your own games

In many ways I consider that having long periods of time to fill, without the aid of external stimuli or the readymade entertainment of television, gives a great impetus to children to devise their own games and entertainments. This necessity to fall back on their own resources can have a constructive outcome and is one of the ways in which cruising can help develop a child's character. Constantly arranging something for the child to do may not always be the best solution, because there is much to be said for a child learning how to occupy himself. There is a real danger in today's world of having our leisure interests packaged and predigested for us, which, along with the bombardment of daily life by radio, television, magazines and advertising, can lead to a loss of the ability to amuse ourselves. Sometimes it might be wiser to stand back and see what the children come up with on their own.

A large collection of battered soft toys of various descriptions from teddy bears to rabbits, horses and monkeys, inhabited our forecabin and gave much warm sustenance to my children. They became almost members of the crew,

Bowriding dolphins are always welcome companions at sea.

particularly one large bear called Yellow Teddy, who lost an eye, an ear and most of his stuffing during his circumnavigation. Doina and Ivan spent hours with these toys, involving them in a variety of imaginary events, writing little plays for them to act out, arranging marriages between them or birthday parties for them. It always seemed to be one or other of the toys' birthdays and a special treat had to be found. Yellow Teddy's birthday became more elaborate each year and involved us adults in present giving, cake making and once even a trip ashore to a restaurant to celebrate his birthday in style.

Some of the plays they devised, mock interviews with toys or the Toyland News, they recorded on a small portable cassette recorder, using different voices for the various toys. This cassette recorder provided hours of entertainment, especially when it came to recording sound effects, which involved a great deal of experimentation. Recording on tape instead of writing is another possibility for schoolwork that is particularly useful on a passage; a recorder can also, of course, be used for playing music or listening to some of the story cassettes especially produced for children.

Stereos and videos

Listening to cassettes is an activity that many children do on passage. The small personal stereos with headphones are popular and a boon if the children's musical tastes are different to one's own, especially as many children do like hearing their favourite pieces over and over and over again! These personal stereos also have the advantage that they can be listened to while lying in one's bunk and so are of great value when the weather is rough or a child feels queasy. When I asked parents what their children did in bad weather, several parents specifically mentioned that their children listened to music or story tapes. The cassettes with stores recorded on them are appreciated by small children as yet unable to read, and even older, reading children still enjoy them, especially if the weather is not so good. It does release the parents from the task of reading stories so they can get on with other jobs.

Similarly, in more recent years, video recordings of favourite films or cartoons have kept young and no-so-young children occupied on passage. There are also innumerable games which can be played on the video monitor, as well as portable video games run on batteries.

Surprises and hidden treats

Tapes are just one of the things that parents buy when they know they are going to make a longer passage. Most parents I have spoken to make various special provisions, buying new toys, books or games. Very often these are put away and produced at intervals during the passage, particularly when boredom sets in. The pleasure of a new toy can create a welcome diversion, especially for smaller children. A longer passage can be marked off into stages, such as the halfway mark, when a celebration and present giving can take place. Small gifts of toys or sweets can be wrapped up and hidden away before the passage.

On our crossing of the Atlantic, which took twenty-six days, we had a little party as we crossed each 10° line, with presents for everyone in the family and a few special goodies to eat. The presents for the children were chosen as items which I thought would keep them occupied for a reasonable length of time – puzzles, colouring books or models to make. After recounting what we had done to a friend in America when we left Maine on the next leg of our voyage down to the Panama Canal and the Pacific, this friend produced a small sack filled with wrapped surprise presents for all of us, and so these parties became a regular feature of all our passages over a week in length. The anticipation of the hidden presents and a special meal also gave the children an added interest in navigation so that they paid close attention to the plotted line creeping across the chart.

The only child

One of the drawbacks to spending a longer time afloat is the lack of contact with other children, and for this reason many parents counsel others to take more than one child to sea if at all possible. Yet many parents sail with a single child quite happily, although invariably they have to devote more time to that child than when there are other children aboard. Especially if the child is young, parents must be prepared to spend a considerable amount of time on passage amusing the child by reading stories or playing games with him. For a shorthanded crew of two, also having to stand night watches and sail the boat, this can be quite tiring. Often father will deal with almost all the boathandling and leave mother to amuse the child, while another solution is to take on an extra crew for longer passages. Older children on their own often devise their own ways of dealing with this singularity. One eight year old lived in his own world, peopled with characters out of his imagination, while according to the parents of another child, who was twelve years old, their son had developed an amazing ability to amuse himself.

Taking it easy

It is on longer passages that the advantage of a separate cabin or area for the children comes into its own. Then their toys and games can be left undisturbed,

Doina and Ivan cool off during a long hot passage in the tropics.

without worrying about tidying up and without overflowing into the rest of the boat. A major tidy-up can easily be carried out when one reaches port. There are few children who are naturally tidy; the vast majority are definitely not, and there is no harm in letting them sleep in a bunk full of their favourite toys if that is what keeps them happy. Being able to shut the door and ignore it all is an easy solution.

Most parents are a little more indulgent on passage than in port, while still respecting the discipline necessary for safety on board. If the children forget to wash or do not get dressed for a few days, it does not matter very much. Taking life easy on a passage has much to recommend it. In practice many children sleep more at sea than they do ashore, and this does not apply only to babies and infants. One of the biggest problems of passage making in fact often occurs on arrival in port, when tired parents are looking forward to a rest and sparkling, thoroughly rested children are full of energy and rearing to go.

The Finishing Point

In the preceding pages I have dealt with various specific topics concerning cruising with children. In this concluding chapter I would like to discuss some general points, such as the drawbacks and benefits of cruising, and to consider particularly the optimum age for taking children on a longer cruise.

In drawing the threads together, I do not want only to give my own opinion but also to present the views of other parents who have cruised extensively with their children. The people who choose to go cruising are, by the nature of this activity, individuals with independent views as varied as the types of boats they cruise in. Nevertheless, having talked to dozens of cruising families, both during the cruising surveys and while cruising myself, some common opinions did emerge, mainly because similar problems have to be dealt with. However, because of the individuality of cruising folk, there are no universal solutions; something that works well for one family does not for others, and everyone must do what suits them best.

When talking to sailing parents about the problems they have encountered, I have been pleasantly surprised by how few these were; as several parents remarked, only the normal problems that one could meet just as easily on land as at sea. Keeping an eye on active small children is one of the major problems that parents mentioned and one I witnessed on *Abuello III* when I was discussing just this subject with Nina Cadle. During our discussion, her three year old daughter Luisa, who we thought was quietly amusing herself in the forecabin, emerged triumphantly covered from head to toe in baby oil, which she had even massaged into her hair.

The difficulty of finding a babysitter to look after small children was also mentioned by parents, although sometimes a teenager from a nearby boat would oblige. My daughter Doina used to look after one year old Brandi Stocks of *Kleena Kleene II*, not so much for the parents to have a night out, but so they could get on with shopping, provisioning, stowing and the preparation of their boat for a passage without Brandi's help.

Where there were two or more children on a boat who were closer in age, there appeared to be fewer problems of this nature as the children played together and amused themselves. On one boat I came across there was a large age difference between two children, which caused constant friction between the elder sister and much younger brother. Although such problems occur ashore as well, they are sometimes magnified on a boat due to the confined space. The lack of other children, even if it is only to fight and disagree with as well as to play with, does affect the sole child on a boat, and the parents themselves have to be prepared to spend more time amusing a lone child.

Living in the confines of a small boat undoubtedly makes family life a much closer affair than on shore, and as Maria van Zelderen, mother of two teenagers, pointed out, 'It is important to share and talk together about any problems the children may have.' Again this advice is equally valid for life ashore. As Dorine Samuelson of *Swan II* said, 'If the parents are happy and enjoy the sailing life, invariably the children are happy and like it too. However, if one parent is not completely happy, this is often reflected in the children.'

All the older cruising children I spoke to had taken long-term cruising in their stride, although one teenage girl did tend to panic when the weather deteriorated and had to be continually reassured by her parents. Even so, she told me that in spite of the problems she would be happy to go on a cruise again if the chance arose. One sixteen year old boy complained that his parents worried too much about him and would not let him take much part in sailing the boat or go on deck, which made long passages particularly boring. This was unusual, because on most cruising boats with older children on board the parents encouraged their children to become proficient sailors.

Most of the problems, such as the lack of other children and the difficulty of education, affect those on a longer voyage more than those on a weekend sail or a short cruise. For children sailing for shorter periods, the benefits to be gained from cruising far outweigh any of the drawbacks. Even so, the majority of parents I have spoken to, who have undertaken a longer voyage, do consider that the voyage benefited their children in various ways, from learning other languages or making new friends to having their eyes opened to the world around them. Most parents thought that their children were more adaptable, independent and self-reliant than if they had lived ashore. But as one parent remarked, 'There is a price to pay for all benefits.'

After eight years and 90,000 miles of cruising on *White Pointer*, the Zelderens are a good example of how successful family life afloat can be.

Marge Bryson of *Ave del Mar*, who had sailed from Alaska to New Zealand, where I spoke to her, balanced the advantages and disadvantages of the voyage for her twelve year old son Stuart. On the negative side she put the fact that Stuart was living an adult life and that he met few children of his own age. This tended to create a social problem for him, because he had become different to other children and always needed a long time to adjust to being with them again. On the positive side she quoted his self-sufficiency and amazing ability to keep himself amused, as well as the fact that he had learnt that one cannot argue with the forces of Nature. Stuart was way ahead of his age in his schoolwork, a common occurrence among sailing children, but Marge was not sure whether or not it was a good thing for a child to be too precocious. Stuart, who was listening to our conversation, agreed that the lack of friends was the greatest drawback to his cruising life, but one that he was quite willing to accept for the excitement of the voyage.

The Faubert family of the French boat *Kouros* had mixed feelings about the benefits of the voyage for their children. For eleven year old Peggy, the voyage had been an adventure on which she had seen many interesting things, and her parents considered her more sociable and outward looking than she had been on shore. They had grave doubts, however, about the wisdom of taking their son Franklin, then four years old, on a voyage that had already lasted two years, feeling he was too young to appreciate it. They also considered that this had forced him into an adult world too early and had thus affected their relationship with him. Another parent who was very aware of this aspect was Bernard Tournier of *Volte*, who counselled: 'It is so easy for a child to become an adult without ever being a child.' The Tourniers had prepared very carefully for cruising with their two young sons, sailing in gentle stages over a couple of summers and waiting for the children to be a little older before setting off on a world voyage.

It is clear that most parents who embark on a longer cruise have thought long and deep about the whole question of taking their children cruising and the optimum time for doing this. There are differing opinions about the best age at which to take children sailing and, although applying particularly to a longer cruise, some of the arguments are equally valid for weekend and holiday sailing. There are basically two schools of thought: those who think that the younger a child is the better, so that he grows up used to life on board and knows little else, and the contrasting view that older children get far more out of sailing and take a wider interest in a voyage.

Younger children do need a lot of attention and supervision; they can rarely be left to their own devices and have to be amused and played with at sea. In return for the effort expended on them, they do not take that much interest in the voyage and the places visited. Many parents specified to me a minimum age of five for taking a child on an extended cruise, as older children are less trouble and appreciate cruising more. With younger children, however, one does not have the task of education, nor do they miss the company of other children quite so much, being more content to spend most of their time in the family atmosphere.

This lack of contact with other children of a similar age and the difficulty of educating children afloat are the two main drawbacks to cruising with older children. The question of education becomes progressively more difficult as the child gets older. Yet most of the teenage children cruising for long periods told me that they willingly trade these drawbacks for the enjoyment they get out of cruising, both the sailing itself, the places they visit and the style of life. As one sixteen year old put it, 'I've got used to my freedom.'

Susanna Graveleau of *Hispania*, who is a teacher of philosophy by profession, put her finger neatly on the whole question of age. 'It's very easy for parents to mistake what is easier for them as being also better for the child.' Without doubt it is harder work for a parent when a child is very small – arranging different meals, constantly supervising and occupying the child. As a child grows up and becomes more independent, life does become progressively easier for the parent. Yet Susanna considers that in spite of all the rich experiences an older child has, the lack of other children's company and a normal school life is detrimental in the long term. Her son Carlos was aged four when I spoke to her and she thought that this was a good age for cruising.

This dilemma of age does have to be thought out when planning a cruise, especially what one is going to do about the question of education. As André Fily of *Stereden Vor* remarked, 'One should know one's child well, and if that child is not motivated to go cruising, then one should seriously reconsider the idea.' This comment was made in respect of an older child, who would have to show some self-discipline in order to tackle schoolwork afloat. All the older children that I have spoken to had clear opinions on this subject, being quite prepared to deal with the difficulties of studying while cruising.

My own opinion is that the optimum age for a lengthy cruise is between the ages of five and thirteen. From about five years old a child is likely to be able to swim, understand safety rules and have some idea what school consists of. These middle childhood years are also the easiest in which to cope with a child's education, whether by correspondence or by oneself. At this age a child is usually less inhibited about making friends quickly in new places than older children, but old enough to remember details and so gain something permanent and lasting from the cruise. These recommendations are for an extended cruise away from home. For family sailing at weekends and on holidays, the younger a child starts to enjoy sailing the better. Teenagers who have been sailing all their lives and grown up on boats make a most welcome crew for anyone.

Whether one sails for a few weeks or several years, there are many things that children can gain from the sailing life. One of the first things they learn is to be self-reliant and to depend on themselves. Foreseeing the consequences of any action taken soon becomes automatic while sailing, as does a proper regard for possible dangers and a respect for the powerful forces of wind and wave. These factors lead children to gain a degree of self-control, consideration of others, and the ability to look outwards from themselves, all of which help them to become responsible and sensible adults. Many sailing children also acquire an enduring love of the sea, which will remain throughout their lives.

Undoubtedly there are problems and difficulties, but these can all be resolved and overcome if the will to do so is there. Cruising with children is much easier than most people imagine. As Jean-Pierre Martin, cruising for five years with his children on *El Djezair*, told me, 'It's very simple to leave, so one shouldn't look for complications.'

It is not the children who make the problems, but sometimes the parents themselves, who exaggerate the difficulties because they are not prepared to cope with them. This point was brought home to me recently at Heathrow Airport in London, when I was returning eleven year old Fabien Bouteleux to his parents in France after a vacation he had spent with our family. At the waiting point for unaccompanied children, a cluster of adults were fussing around their charges prior to handing them over to the stewardess, making the children nervous and fidgety. Fabien, world traveller that he is with a six year voyage on *Calao* behind

There is a solution for everything, even Christmas in the sunshine.

him, looked on quite relaxed and unperturbed about his impending flight, clearly wondering what all the commotion was about. He showed the confidence and independence that is typical of cruising children.

Children have often accompanied their parents into a new life, as in the days of pioneering or settling new lands, demonstrating their capacity for resourcefulness and adaptability. In many circumstances children have shown that they will take almost anything in their stride, adapt to a new situation or enjoy the adventure of an activity such as sailing. It is the adults who fuss and worry, not the children. Some of these worries are indeed real and parents are right to consider them, but there is nothing that cannot be overcome with a little thought, effort and careful planning. There is absolutely no reason for making the children one's excuse for not going cruising.

Index

abdominal pain 54, 60–1
Abuelo III 28, 93, 102
analgesics 61–2
antibiotics 52, 53, 60
appendicitis 60
athletes foot 58
Ave del Mar 104
Aventura 12, 14, 17, 65

backpack 71
bath 39, 41
bathing platform 16, 32
bed-wetting 56–7
bleeding 47, 48
books 12, 18, 54, 94
boarding ladder 16, 32
Bouteleux, Muriel, Erick, Sidonie
   & Fabien 25, 106
breastfeeding 56, 57
Bryson, Marge & Stuart 104
buoyancy aid 25, 27–30, 41, 43,
   44
burns 35, 49–50

cabin
   aft 13
   children's 17, 66
   fore 12, 17, 66
Calao 25, 106
carrycot 11, 15, 32, 64, 65, 70, 71
Christopher Robin 73
cockpit
   central 13, 14
   protection 21, 71

companionway 16, 17
constipation 55–6, 61
cooker 35
cooking gas 35
Curt, Madeli 24, 26

dinghy 16, 18, 30–2, 33, 79, 87–8
diarrhoea 55, 56, 67
diet 62–3
diving 33, 87
dolphins 21, 84–6, 98

El Djezair 16, 106
environment 4, 5, 86

fathers 4
family life 4–5
Faubert family 104
fear 5
Fily, André 106
first aid 46, 47
   kit 51–3
   manual 46–7
Fiu 24
flags 76, 82
Fletcher, Max & Christopher 73
floating 42
French, Sylvia, Ian & John 72
friendship 6, 104

galley 17, 78–9
games 12, 14, 17, 18, 93, 94–7
grabrails 15, 17
Graveleau, Susan & Carlos 105

Hancock, Ian, Derry & Eric   13, 68
Hantel, Benedict & Eric   14, 31
harnesses   21–3, 37
hatchway   22
heatstroke   57
helming   15, 77
Hispania   105
Holmes, Vicky & John   72–3
Horizon   5

immunisation   50
independence   3, 5
infections   46, 58, 59–61
    ear   59
    eye   59
insect bites   51, 58, 62
Iron Butterfly   13

jellyfish   33

kerosene   35
Kleena Kleene II   11, 66, 71, 103
Korong II   72–3
knots   76
Kouros   104

Lanoue, Fred   42
leecloths   65
lice   59
lifejackets   21, 23, 25, 27–30, 33, 37, 44
lifelines   15, 22

Macdonald, Liz, Bruce & Jeff   5
Martin, Jean-Pierre   106
malaria   50, 51
medicines   34
mosquito netting   51
multihulls   14

nappies   11, 68–9

navigation   78, 91
netting   15, 25, 64, 66
Newman, Virginia   38

outboard engine   30–2

pain   54, 61–2
panic   5, 34
Pitteloud, Françoise & Kevin   73
planning   2
poliomyelitis   50
Pomona   72
pushchair   11, 64, 70
Pytheas   14

radio   53, 66, 78
reading   79, 93
resuscitation   47–8
Ribes, Nina, Juan & Luisa   28, 93, 102
rig   14
rowing   30
Runestaff   68

safety, water   2, 33–4
sailboard   87–8
sailhandling   15, 76, 77, 90
Samuelson, Nicky   38
schoolwork   13, 90
seasickness   14, 54–5, 56, 89, 90
sedative   62
sharks   33, 34
shells   33, 83, 84
shock   50
sling   32, 70
spray dodger   14, 15, 21
steering position   15
Stereden Vor   106
Stocks, Bill, Frances & Brandi   11, 65, 66, 71
stonefish   33
storage   17, 1 8

Index

Svanhild   4
Swan II   38, 103
swimming pool   40, 41

tetanus   50
threadworms   59
Timmermans, Claire   38
Tournier, Bernard   105
toys   12, 14, 17, 18, 40, 54, 66, 93, 101

unconsciousness   47, 57

Vahine Rii   38
van Zelderen family   13, 103, 104
video   94, 99
vitamins   63, 68
Volte   105

Warna Carina   12
watchkeeping   77, 90
water, fresh   18, 69
whales   84–6
wheelhouse   14, 21
White Pointer   13, 103, 104
winches   15, 77